Short Voyages to the Land of the People

utopia

PHILOSOPHY POLITICAL THEORY AESTHETICS

Judith Butler and Frederick M. Dolan
EDITORS

Short Voyages to the Land of the People

JACQUES RANCIÈRE

Translated by JAMES B. SWENSON

STANFORD UNIVERSITY PRESS
STANFORD, CALIFORNIA
2003

Assistance for the translation was provided by
the French Ministry of Culture.

Short Voyages to the Land of the People was originally published
in French in 1990 under the title *Courts voyages au pays du peuple*,
© 1990, Éditions du Seuil.

Stanford University Press
Stanford, California

English translation © 2003 by the Board of Trustees
of the Leland Stanford Junior University.
All rights reserved.

Printed in the United States of America
on acid-free, archival-quality paper.

Library of Congress Cataloging-in-Publication Data

Rancière, Jacques.
  [Courts voyages au pays du peuple. English]
  Short voyages to the land of the people / Jacques Rancière ;
translated by James B. Swenson.
    p.   cm. — (Atopia : philosophy, political theory, aesthetics)
  ISBN 0-8047-3681-2 (cloth : alk. paper)
  ISBN 0-8047-3682-0 (pbk. :alk. paper)
  1. Voyages, Imaginary.   2. Utopias.   3. Reality in literature.
4. Women in literature.   5. Proletariat in literature.
I. Title.   II. Series: Atopia (Stanford, Calif.)
PN56.V59R3613 2003
843'.914—DC18

2002156075

Original Printing 2003
Last figure below indicates year of this printing:
12   11   10   09   08   07   06   05   04   03
Designed by Janet Wood
Typeset by Tim Roberts in 10/12 Minion

Contents

Introduction 1

The New Land 7

   The Poet's Voyage 9

   The Territory of Utopia 25

   The People's Song 41

   The Mirror of the Sea 56

The Poor Woman 67

   The Petrified Flower 69

   Marthe and René 86

A Child Kills Himself 105

   Notes 135

Introduction

This is a book about voyages. Not so much to far-off isles or exotic vistas as to those much closer lands that offer the visitor the image of another world. Just across the straits, away from the river, off the beaten path, at the end of the subway line, there lives another people (unless it is, quite simply, the people). We are offered the unexpected spectacle of another humanity in its many figures: the return to origins, the descent to the netherworld, the arrival in the promised land. The July sunshine dappling the tree leaves becomes, for the English poet on a walking tour of the Continent, the new light of revolutionary France wedded to festive nature. The clinking of glasses in an inn along the Saône, the cool of a June evening, the harmony of voice and violin on a Sunday afternoon in the country become the fraternal communion of a new society. And without even leaving his house, the historian discovers in the maid he has seduced the soul of the rustics and barbarians who made France.

But we do not need the villages to be cheerful, the sun

shining, or the maid pretty in order to enjoy the voyage. The dull gray of a winter sky upon concrete apartment blocks or the corrugated tin roofs of a shantytown can fulfill the traveler if it presents him with what he has long sought and can immediately recognize, in its very foreignness, as just like what he has already spoken, read, heard, and dreamed: the proletariat in person. Such was the flower, its living reality just waiting to be plucked, that a certain text of Mao Zedong's promised to those who agreed to go out, leaving behind books and cities, and get down off their horses. There it was: reality, denouncing the vanity of books and yet just like what the books led us to expect, what words led us to love. More than the analysis of oppression or the sense of duty toward the oppressed, the core political experience of our generation may well have been to go on such a voyage, discovering for ourselves this recognizable foreignness, this shimmering of life. The questions we will pose here will concern, first, the signs by which a gaze—curious, nonchalant, or impassioned—comes to recognize reality as exemplary of the idea; and second, the way in which a thought comes to incarnate itself, in a landscape or a living scene, in order to make a concept present.

In this book will be found a few voyages chosen by chance or affinity, a few brief encounters or missed appointments that are part of the archaeology of this politics: voyages of missionaries in search of the people of the future, tourists who come across this people by chance, or a proletarian who never meets them but nonetheless finds the unexpected mirror of his condition in the South Seas. Above all, foreigners will pass through this book: an English poet surprised by the festivals of the French Revolution on his path to the Alps; a German poet who meets and mocks a French utopian who has lost his way in Strasbourg, before himself going off to dig an abyss beneath the good, scientific revolution; another German poet who puts his song of poverty at the mercy of the obscure desire of a Parisian working girl; a Swedish actress who incarnates, for an Italian film director, the society woman whose visit to the unknown people restores her foreignness.

Under their gaze, to the rhythm of their steps, the images of the new world come into being and pass away. This is not simply because the foreigner comes to know the language or because experience disillusions his gaze. Lucidity only provides another way of drawing the landscape, of creating an agreement between its lines and shadows and the habits of belief. It is not because the aridity of stone and the cold of the tomb impose themselves where, before, the flowers of the festive people and the happy future had been offered. It is also because the foreigner—the naif, it will be said, he who is not yet informed—persists in the curiosity of his gaze, displaces his angle of vision, reworks the first way of putting together words and images, undoes the certainties of place, and thereby reawakens the power present in each of us to become a foreigner on the map of places and paths generally known as reality. Thus the foreigner loosens what he had bound together. The poet who put together the words and images uniting the play of light and cloud with the sensible certainties of politics revolts against the impoverishment of the image, takes back his words, takes his place in the gap between images and any promise of common happiness. Thus diverge two paths: that of one who continues to recognize in the land he crosses the words and places of the book, and the path of one who takes back his words and figures, engraves the flower in the hardness of stone or in a poem, in the rediscovered foreignness of the work [*œuvre*].

These pages are thus not written for those who believe that foreigners are naive, that voyages are only good for educating youth before youth fades, and that reality is suitable for denouncing the clouds of utopia. What will be seen here instead is how the mirage or utopian madness represents a minuscule excess with respect to the procedures that positive knowledge and reasonable politics use to construct reality, the procedures that put together words and images so as to produce the point of coincidence, the truly utopian point: the wordless evidence of the thing given in itself, the exact coincidence of word and thing. For the spectacle of reality disillusions the missionaries of utopia only very rarely. More often they go back home because they are tired of walking so much. And those who keep going succumb more often to the wounds inflicted by words than to the weight of things. Thus those who believe in the resistance of the real and continue to be surprised that men can live and die for words have little to teach us about the bitter knowledge of travel. Their own science is that of sharing the utopian point, calling it reality, society, or some other name less embarrassing than Icaria. They thus work to assure the means of peace, which are certainly precious but are not thereby entitled to be called the paths of truth. To know a bit more about the threads that trace the ordinary ways and forgotten paths of utopia, it would be better to follow the labor of the poets, putting together the words that mark the quest for a place and the scansion of its absence: Wordsworth, Büchner, and Rilke, who travel throughout these pages, Baudelaire digging in their margins, and all those who set out on the voyage of words never to return, hanging until the final leap on the improbability and unpredictability of an encounter, "the union of a long sentence with a bit of reality that it is not."[1]

The New Land

The Poet's Voyage

In the great book of culture and its "selected works," William Wordsworth has gone down as the poet of lakes, cuckoos, and daffodils. A poet of nature walks, who, a critic of our own century will say, needed to make a few trips to the tropics to understand what nature means.[1] But we need not speak of the tropics. His younger brothers—Keats, Shelley, and Byron—went off to die on the shores of Greece and Italy between their twenty-sixth and thirty-seventh years. William Wordsworth, meanwhile, found his South and his Orient on the shores of Lake Como. And he died an octogenarian in his own country.

He was not always indifferent to those fevers of the age that drew his younger brothers to the lands where poetry and freedom were born. Only he was lucky enough to have been born earlier, to be twenty years old in 1790, when on a clear day the land of ancient freedom could be seen from the white cliffs of Dover.

Thus it was that he twice crossed the Channel and visited the land of the Revolution. The first time it was in passing and without any political intent. At most, his joy in a first escape from student life, far from the gray halls and dried laurels of college, his desire to see higher mountains and wider lakes than those of his native Cumberland, made him an accomplice of the great enthusiasm for the new freedom. To leave enough time to tour the Alps and be back home before winter, he and his companion landed at Calais on July 13, 1790.

There was a festival the next day in Calais, as in all of France. More precisely, it was the Festival of all revolutionary festivals: the festival of the Federation, the apogee of the great dream of the pacific and fraternal revolution.

Everywhere on their path the two friends met the actors and settings of the ongoing celebration. A piece of luck— their lot—says the poet. This was not what he had come for. "Nature" alone was then "sovereign" in his heart.

But was that not precisely the sovereignty celebrated on those July days, mixing in the traveler's sight the flowers and harvests of summer with those of the Revolution? Particularly in an age of great walking tours, such touristic outings were far more apt than doctrinal propaganda for communicating revolutionary enthusiasm. Quite naturally, without any violence in action or in speech, without any staging of allegories or confrontation of arguments. What is immediately evident will always win out over what is proved by argument. And how could one not feel, the whole length of the trip, the sensible reality of the concept? How could one not associate within a single emotion all the cheerful spectacles of nature and of village life that give the people's festival its artless emblems: the July sun seen from the shade of trees, the flowers decorating triumphal arches, the garlands on window sills, the rustling of leaves in the light breeze, the dances of freedom beneath a starry sky, the welcoming smile on faces lit by a joy shared with millions of brothers, and in the most remote villages,

> benevolence and blessedness,
> Spread like a fragrance everywhere, when spring
> Hath left no corner of the earth untouched.[2]

Spring in the month of July: a time of beginning that is also a time of fulfillment. The land of the Revolution is lit by neither the hesitant sun of early spring nor by the brutal glare of a heat wave. The calm certainty of new happiness is given in the play of sun and cloud. The neutral light of overcast skies and the flattening light of full summer are equally unsuited to this organization of the visible that so charms the vision of the walkers: the precise outline of landscapes and scenes, the self-evidence, with neither lack nor excess, of these vignettes of the naturally happy people framed by the play of the sun piercing through clouds and trees, attesting the evidence of a fulfillment.

> Not in Utopia, subterranean fields,
> Or some secreted island, Heaven knows where!
> But in the very world, which is the world
> Of all of us.[3]

Students on vacation amid a festive people. The peaceful river of happy revolutions. After having reached Chalon on foot, the travelers now glide down the waters of the Saône between slopes laden with vines. They give themselves completely over to the happiness of moving to the same rhythm as the people on march, of being foreigners no more, in a country where the only foreigners are the enemies of human happiness:

> Clustered together with a merry crowd
> Of those emancipated, a blithe host
> Of travellers, chiefly delegates returning
> From the great spousals newly solemnised
> At their chief city, in the sight of Heaven ...
>   In this proud company
> We landed—took with them our evening meal,
> Guests welcome almost as the angels were
> To Abraham of old. The supper done,
> With flowing cups elate and happy thoughts
> We rose at signal given, and formed a ring
> And, hand in hand, danced round and round the board;
> All hearts were open, every tongue was loud
> With amity and glee.[4]

The day after this communion of a summer's eve, the travelers left the delegates of the people on march for the solitude of the Chartreuse, the majesty of Mount Blanc, and the "Abyssinian" splendor of Como. Then, through Switzerland, Germany, and Belgium, the poet went back to the benches of the university, skirting around the country of freedom that he had just crossed, he tells us, "as a bird moves through the air" or as a fish "feeds in its proper element."[5]

But perhaps he is being too modest. It is not simply his

youthful insouciance that makes him take the light air of a summer's wandering for the element of freedom and the radiance of a new world. It is not only the landscape lit by the contrasts of shadow and light that is transformed into a political self-evidence. The effects and oppositions of politics also present themselves in the contrast of landscapes, casting the shadow of servitude on the splendid slopes of Savoy, highlighting the jubilation of free Switzerland on the heights of the Valais. In the most remote hamlet the traveler could see the shadow cast by far-off tyranny. Conversely, he could see nature smiling on the mountain village showered with freedom's blessings:

> *Heart*-blessings—outward treasures too which the eye
> Of the sun peeping through the clouds can spy,
> And every passing breeze will testify.
> There, to the porch, belike with jasmine bound
> Or woodbine wreaths, a smoother path is wound;
> The housewife there a brighter garden sees,
> Where hum on busier wing her happy bees;
> On infant cheeks there fresher roses blow;
> And grey-haired men look up with livelier brow,—
> To greet the traveler needing food and rest.[6]

Others might be content with such happy stopovers. But the following fall the young graduate sets out again for France. It is another sort of trip:

> But now, relinquishing the scrip and staff,
> And all enjoyment which the summer sun
> Sheds round the steps of those who meet the day.[7]

In principle, the voyage is a linguistic one: the young man claims that he has come to perfect his French in order to become a guide and interpreter for tourists of high rank. Such, at least, is the reason he must have given his austere tutors to justify a prolonged sojourn on the banks of the Loire, in the garden of France. But the wintry light of this garden illuminates a scene that is no longer a pastoral idyll. In Orléans and Blois, he encountered the rigidity of the old society of aristocrats, officers, and notables. In learning the language and its idioms, he came to understand the reasons and debates of the Revolution, whose songs and garlands were all he had known about it before. And the spectacle of nature itself suffers the division of the landscape that had charmed the tourist. In the midst of the greenery of meadows, near a joyous brook, a wrecked and roofless convent, victim of revolutionary passion, moves not the believer but the traveler, for whom the cross atop the steeple, the bell that once rang matins or angelus announced hospitality and peaceful rest: not merely the restoration of the walker's forces but the welcome of a new spectacle in the immemorial certainty of the hours and seasons of nature.

Nevertheless, in opposition to the now mute sign of welcome, living testimonies give meaning to the battle. Another image is substituted for the pain of the razed steeple: the intact pomp of former royal residences. In this imperious decor the sufferings of the old world and the combats of the new world appear clearly, making manifest what one is fighting against and why one must fight: the hunger-bitten face of a peasant girl who is shuffling along to the languid gait of a famished heifer tied to her arm by a cord; the courage of the citizens and the suppressed tears of the women at the call of the fatherland in danger. The impression made by these passing spectacles cannot be effaced by any change in the light. They are reasons become flesh and blood, marks of a truth sent by heaven itself to prove the cause good and pure,

> which no one could stand up against,
> Who was not lost, abandoned, selfish, proud,
> Mean, miserable, wilfully depraved,
> Hater perverse of equity and truth.[8]

But perhaps all that—the stigmata of oppression like the fervor of patriotic volunteers—counts less than the fraternal hand that points them out to the traveler. In fact, the poet has found a new walking companion, the young officer Michel Beaupuy, who has renounced the privileges of his birth to serve the republican cause. The gaze of this young officer, who has deserted the caste of the nobility without having left behind aristocratic virtues, now provides the principle, the contrasted light that makes the world's spectacles sensible to the young foreigner. In him are incarnated the ancient virtues that the new world has rediscovered; in him is reflected the fugitive emotion of the landscapes through which the vacationing students once passed. This captain who breathes out the sweetness of "aromatic flowers on Alpine turf," despite the persecution of his peers, also moves through the great events of the times as if through the pages of a picture book,

> an old romance, or tale
> Of Fairy, or some dream of actions wrought
> Behind the summer clouds.[9]

Thus is offered the countenance of a strange cultural revolution: the transference of the duties of monastic priesthood and the marks of honor customary to men and women of quality to the laboring and suffering people. The courtesy that this revolutionary pays to "the homely in their homely works" indeed resembles not only the religious service of divine love, but also

A passion and a gallantry, like that
Which he, a soldier, in his idler day,
Had paid to woman.[10]

The noble officer of the popular Revolution—a figure of the reconciliation of the old and the new, of heroic war and peaceful love, of the simplicity of nature and the distinction of nobility—deploys around himself the contours of a visibility that fixes the same evidence that the furtive sun allowed to be glimpsed through the summer clouds. The promise of a reconciliation is traced behind the light self-evidence of happiness and the painful self-evidence of injustice and combat. Nature, beyond the trial of justice and war in which she is completely engaged, will emerge more than ever in her inherent state, her primordial peace. The trial endured and the reconciliation promised are incarnated with the greatest possible evidence in the speech of he whom nature has consecrated, he whom nature has called to embody in action the deep sense of the age, to give it an outward shape, that of a new benediction for the world. It is a new mode of truth's existence that then imposes itself on the gaze of the foreigner:

Then doubt is not, and truth is more than truth,—
A hope it is, and a desire; a creed
Of zeal, by authority Divine
Sanctioned, of danger, difficulty, or death.[11]

Just as summer's clouds produced the revolutionary surreality of nature, the mission embodied in the vision, gesture, and voice of the hero produces the sur-truth of battle. Thus is attested the living hope of seeing injustice and error vanish and the dispersed populations unite in one body: not a Leviathan submitted to an imperious head and a regulated interplay of organs, but a supple and harmonious form of the multiple, resembling the clouds stretched out across the summer sky. Thus Attica can live once again on the banks of the Loire, where the officer and the poet dream of a "philosophic war, led by philosophers," like the one that made the companions of Dion, Plato's royal disciple, set sail for Syracuse.

But what makes for the happiness of the sojourn also makes for its risk. The departure for the war front of he whose face reflected the certainty of nature in revolution may be all that is needed for the synthesis to come undone and for everything to fall apart: words and images, reasons to love and reasons to fight, the clouds of politics and those of a summer sky.

It is also a question of location. In the fall of 1792, the poet left Orléans for Paris, where he arrived immediately following the September massacres. For the foreigner, the conquered Tuileries, the empty Carrousel, and the Temple where the royal prisoner was jailed were images of a book that was certainly memorable but that was closed to his understanding. Above all, the Revolution that in Orléans or Blois clearly confronted the old order was divided against itself in the metropolis. Was the war to blame or was it the fanaticism of the sectarians who were propelling the Terror? Or was it the very space of the revolutionary city, in which the noise of speech and the agitation of factions did not allow the people's achievement [*l'œuvre populaire*] to be reflected in the landscapes and spectacles of a new world? Already, a year before, during his first passage through Paris, the traveler had felt the powerlessness of the setting of the Bastille in ruins to fulfill the promise of the unheard-of event. Sunlight with no shadows and the silent winds composed a landscape that left the imagination bereft of its expectations. And opposed to the mute relics of the people's work was the strange force of an image preserved from the old order:

> Where silent zephyrs sported with the dust
> Of the Bastille, I sate in the open sun,
> And from the rubbish gathered up a stone,
> And pocketed the relic, in the guise
> Of an enthusiast; yet, in honest truth,
> I looked for something that I could not find,
> Affecting more emotion than I felt;
> For 'tis most certain, that these various sights,
> However potent their first shock, with me
> Appeared to recompense the traveller's pains
> Less than the painted Magdalene of Le Brun,
> A beauty exquisitely wrought, with hair
> Dishevelled, gleaming eyes, and rueful cheek
> Pale and bedropped with everflowing tears.[12]

THE NEW LAND 19

The comparison between the mute stones of the people's work and the eloquent tears on the face of the courtesan is too beautiful not to have been invented after the fact. The hair and tears of the sinner are spread less in the painting saved from the destruction of the Carmelites than in the verses of the *Prelude*. Twelve years stand between these memories and a poet who has abandoned his youthful illusions and whose heart now dances only to the rhythm of armies of daffodils. Back in a homeland at war against France, made despondent by the Terror and the transformation of revolutionary war into a war of conquest, momentarily tempted to transfer the fading enthusiasm for these armies-of-freedom-become-armies-of-oppression into the enterprise of individual and moral liberation proclaimed by Godwin, the poet had already drawn the lessons of the journey in a play written in 1797, *The Borderers*, whose plot and moral are inspired by Schiller's *The Robbers*. The leader of the band of avengers, Mortimer, allows himself to be deceived and led to crime by the sophisms of the diabolical Rivers, who knows the sovereign art of finding the seed of evil in every good action and the promise of justice in every criminal action. The moral of this story, which is situated on the Scottish borderlands in the age of the Crusades, does not simply teach us that ends do not justify all means. More strangely and seriously, it shows us that crime is virtually present from the moment that the self-evidence of nature is split in the couple of ends and means. The human judgment that should control this relation is incapable of sustaining it. Opposed to the play of sun and shadow in the revolutionary sky is this pure scene of dialectical artifice, this heath in mourning for the signs of happiness, justice, and promise. The philosophical soldier can point out to his companion no landscape of festival and battle, no spectacle of suffering or arrogance. Justice has entirely passed into the unanswerable speech of the sophist, who has crossed "the visible barriers of the world / and traveled into things to come."[13] And to his companion in arms, who sings the praises of the sword raised to defend innocence, Mortimer responds with the image of a world bereft of all innocence:

> We look
> But at the surface of things, we hear
> Of towns in flames, fields ravaged, young and old
> Driven out in flocks to want and nakedness,
> Then grasp our swords and rush upon a cure
> That flatters us, because it asks not thought.
> The deeper malady is better hid—
> The world is poisoned at the heart.[14]

Here is an answer to Huxley's irony. No doubt a voyage to the tropics would have taught the poet that nature is not the pastoral idyll of temperate Europe, that nature is alien, inhuman, and diabolical. But it might be better to follow to the end of their path the golden clouds of the revolutionary landscape, in order to recognize, in the coming-apart of the image, the more radical foreignness of an evil that no liberator's sword can touch. Is it not in order to bear witness to this, better than any discourse could do, that the penitent and provocative Magdalene spreads forth her long hair and silk garments in the great drama of redemption?

No doubt this image is also a symptom. The biographers ended up learning the carefully hidden secret of this eight-thousand-verse autobiography: the love affair between the foreigner and the young Annette Vallon, and the abandonment of her and the couple's love child on the banks of the Loire. Then the exemplary stories can flourish, in which remorse provokes the poet's political apostasy, which in turn explains the decline of his inspiration before even half his life was done.

Still, this apostasy and decline have a strange aspect. Doubtless the time (to the end of the 1840s) that the old poet, having returned to order and morality, took to correct a work pretty much finished before 1810 testifies to a loss of inspiration. But how can we not admire the care that the devout old Tory took to rewrite the verses of the young enthusiast, to make the contrasting landscapes of freedom and oppression more lively and convincing? What is at work in this rewriting is assuredly something more profound than the disillusionment of the revolutionary, the remorse of the guilty lover, or even the renewed tenderness of an old man for the illusions of his youth. What the poet traces in this rewriting is the separation of the paths of the future. The joyless return to social and moral order first passes through the point where the poet, conscious of his mission, bids farewell to the revolutionary tourist, the point where no possible identification can be made between the movements of the clouds in the summer sky and the political rumor of servitude and liberation. Nature bears witness to no avenger; its spectacles symbolize no future for the community. Like Rivers in *The Borderers*, the revolutionaries of politics and morality falsely believed that they had traveled beyond the visible barriers of the world into things to come. The price of this illusory voyage is their consenting to a crime, a crime that takes on the insistent figure of abandonment. Rivers has constructed his morality of the future to justify having abandoned a captain falsely accused by his sailors on a desert isle in the sea off the coast of Palestine. And in the name of justice he pushes Mortimer to the same crime. Persuaded by Rivers that the father of the woman he loves has usurped his paternity, the avenger will abandon the blind old man to the mortal hazards of the heath with neither guide nor food. As the price of this crime, Mortimer will condemn himself to wandering without speech and without hope of hospitality—the wandering of a being without a name. For having left a child on the banks of the Loire, the poet will learn that the future of politicians is always the forgetting of an abandonment more fundamental than all the ills of which they promise to rid the earth. He will learn that the poet can cross the barriers of the visible and travel into things that do not yet exist, but only on the condition of untying the knot that once bound the course of his journey to the spectacle of liberation, of undoing the synthesis figured in the spring-summer sky of the Revolution. He will have to leave the army of clouds to its silent march toward the abyss in which they are forever reborn before vanishing once again, like power, glory, and empire, to follow his own path:

> A humble walk
> Here is my body doomed to tread, this path,

A little hoary line and faintly traced,
Work, shall we call it, of the shepherd's foot
Or of his flock?—joint vestige of them both.[15]

Wordsworth's path is the poetry of the humble, dedicated to glorifying, in the language of the simple, the most modest of wildflowers that the walker ignores or steps on. A task of protection, or better of rehabilitation, of consideration for all that is too small, too humble, too much a child not to be subject to the rigors of abandonment. This is assuredly what unites the poet's own invention—the new lyricism of simple things—to the emotions of the young enthusiast. It is also why the old man who has returned to order still takes up the pen to combat the humiliating dispositions of the Poor Law, to contrast to its paternalistic intentions the singular pride of a pair of migrant laborers, who for four years trailed with them from lodging to lodging the body of their dead child rather than abandon it to burial at the cost of the parish.[16]

The poet takes care of the dead child that every politics abandons: the little Lucy Gray of the ballad, who, lamp in hand, has gone off to seek her mother in the snow storm and whose footprints come to an end at the riverbank; the two dead siblings that the child of "We are Seven" obstinately includes in counting her family; the boy whose story symbolically opens the *Poems of the Imagination*, clambering up the cliff to call to the owls who respond from the other side of the valley.[17] The child whom nature answers dies before the end of his twelfth year, because, of course, a being whom nature answers cannot exist. However naively pantheistic we may think him to be, the poet knows that nature does not respond to poets any more than to revolutionaries or even children, at least those who stay alive. The poet speaks on the tomb of the child who spoke with the birds about wisdom and night. The poem is the future of the one whose traces end at the water's edge, the preserved life of the child who had to die, the crossing within the realm of the visible of the barrier of the visible. More than to the poor girl dragging the weight of enslaved labor along the roads of France, and more, even, than to the little girl abandoned on the banks of the Loire, who will grow up well and marry honorably, the poet owes his fidelity to the child who can survive himself only in death. Along with a few refrains on daffodils, cuckoos, and celandine, he will leave this future to posterity.

It matters little, then, that he should have lacked inspiration at the end. He fixed for the future a scene that will not be forgotten. Future times will not cease to oppose to the pickaxe of demolition the face of the sinner, the eternally upsetting presence of a gratification and an evil irreducible to the sufferings and redemptions of the political and social order, an image destined to go on doubling the virile images of free people and reconciled nature. And the poets of the future will never be done with drawing all the figures of the dead child that every politics abandons. Emblems of the impossible revolution or relics of a revolution, always beyond the pickaxe of demolition and the trowel of new building. The enigma of the woman, the passion of the child, the mission of the artist.

The Territory of Utopia

Could it be that the new world, once and for all, had chosen the site of its manifestation and the time of its celebrations? The horse-drawn barge gliding from Chalon to Lyons, the vines ripening in summer's first heat, the plucking of the violins, the songs and dances that, on an evening or a Sunday afternoon, in Burgundian inns and granges, bring together those separated by the hazard of birth: for images of love, images of fecundity. In this month of June 1833, the Saint-Simonian *compagnons* of the "mission of the East" are living a dream.[18] From the labors and marches of their mornings to the preaching and songs of their evenings, none of their acts or meetings fails to mark an event and form a symbol, none of their accents fails to find its resonance in the harmonies of day and night. This is what it means to be an *apostle*: not simply to preach and work for the good of the laboring and suffering people, but to sanctify every one of their labors and pleasures, the gestures and the tools of their tasks, the earth watered by their sweat, the sky that brings it to fruition.

It must be admitted that this idyll is the recompense for a voyage that so far has not spread many rose petals beneath the apostles' feet. Six months ago the first detachment of the "pacific army of laborers" left Paris, not without a few stones being thrown at them as they passed Charenton. It was an eminently symbolical departure: on November 28, 1832, the head of the Saint-Simonian religion, Father Enfantin, entered Sainte-Pélagie prison to serve a six-month term. And the same day, at the same hour, the first Saint-Simonian detachment left Paris, the city of bourgeois prostitution, for Lyon, the exemplary city of working-class labor and struggle. Their mission was to raise, by the force of speech and example, the battalions of an unprecedented army, setting out to battle the industrial future with the same passion and discipline that the armies of the Revolution and the Empire had when they set out for the conquest of Europe.

To accomplish this task the missionaries had to go *commune* with the workers: to transform in practice the habits and thoughts that constantly reproduced their privileged life as bourgeois *docteurs*; to make known, concretely, to laborers caught between the egotistical routine of survival and the upheavals of revolutionary violence, the Saint-Simonian doctrine of industry and love. They must go "live as proletarians" [*faire du prolétariat*] and "consecrate labor" [*installer le travail*].

The connection of the two tasks implies a certain hierarchy. To make themselves known to the proletariat, they must first know the proletariat as a life experience. Thus they set out to *faire du prolétariat*: no longer merely working with their hands as they did in their community at Ménilmontant, where, despite having dismissed all their servants and taken brooms or rakes into their own hands, they nonetheless continued to live like bourgeois upon the inheritance of the most fortunate among them, but living from the labor of their hands, receiving the "baptism of wages": a sacrament different from a simple initiation of the bourgeois into working-class life. For even the "true" proletarians in the Saint-Simonian family must be rebaptized, transforming what had been merely the chance of a condition into a priesthood. The former butcher's boy Desloges, who had done all different kinds of work before being employed by the apostles as a laborer at the *Globe* and then as a concierge at Ménilmontant, just like the engineer Hoart, the musician Rogé, or the student Mangin, must receive this baptism of a new life in which the word becomes flesh and labor only insofar as labor becomes speech and manifestation. Even the silk worker Augier will symbolically leave the city of Lyon, where he has always exercised this profession that others come to discover, in order to manifest the new work [*œuvre nouvelle*] on a construction site in Grenoble.

The voyage of labor is thus a transformation of self and a manifestation for others. The whole problem lies in the relation between the two. The choice of a kind of work in Lyon is also the choice of an element of baptism: the water of circulation or the fire of production. Choosing water means prolonging in the work of labor at Lyon the mission that had been given to the travelers on the road from Paris to Lyon: to circulate everywhere—through speech but also through song, spectacles, costume, the red beret, and the medallion of the Father—the rumor, refrains, and images of the new world. That they may accomplish this the voyagers should "engage in conversation the drivers, horsemen, boatmen, postmasters, and mistresses," even select "one or two fellows who travel with the boatmen of Chalon or the Rhône," in order to be in constant contact with "those who see the most people and carry the news."[19] An industry of travel and communication that immerses characters in the cold winter waters and puts the missionaries at the heart of the unknown networks and obscure forces of the hidden land.

This naturally was the choice made by the head of the "Fourth Detachment," Cayol. This former deckhand, merchant in Marseilles, and republican roughneck could not resist the call of the water and the universe of sailors. He thus makes preparations for leading a group of barges to Arles: "Until now I have only sailed on salt water and an excursion on the Rhône . . . could give me a first practical idea of river navigation. An excellent thing for an apostle to know." He had already placed one of his men among a group of sailors building barges. And more could have been hired. But it is at this point that his plan conflicted with the elements: "Sent to Perrache . . . he meets only men who love fire better than water."[20]

These men of fire, just as naturally, are the adepts of the two artillery captains, Hoart and Bruneau. In resigning from the army to join the Saint-Simonian family, these polytechnicians did not thereby renounce the grand ideals of military democracy: the apprenticeship of classes and baptism by fire. "To organize labor, one must be a laborer, just as, to organize an army, one must have braved rifle shot and cannon fire."[21] One must inspire confidence in the workers one wishes to enroll, and in order to do this candidate officers must show their practical capacity to workers who, even when they gladly solicit the speech of the Saint-Simonians, still think that they are in the workshop "just for show."[22] But above all, this heterogeneous troop, in which the bourgeois dedicating his leisure to the people's cause mixes with the worker seduced by the adventure that takes him away from proletarian routine, must be stabilized and transformed, both for its sake and for that of the workers who observe it. All must learn or relearn the constraints and regularities of the working day and liquidate the parasitic ideologies that are discreetly maintained by devotion to variable hours and the community of goods of the militant family. The fire of production, of the army, and of purification, which the two captains seek for themselves and for their troops in the world of the forge, must also, in the eyes of the workers, attest the glory of the new apostolate. It is not a matter of the missionaries reeducating themselves through proletarian discipline and merging, for the sake of propaganda, into the anonymity of the working masses. To rehabilitate labor in the eyes of the bourgeois and make the proletarians conscious of labor's *pacific* power, the apostle, clothed in Saint-Simonian costume and bearing his name on his breast, should on the contrary make manifest his double nature, the miracle of his transfiguration: "Bourgeois transformed into laborers, what an unheard-of metamorphosis! Who can deny the power of love of he who inspired it! Who can deny that God is there!"[23]

But the proof of God's existence is one thing and the miracle of his sensible presence another. The apostles will quickly learn this lesson. It is not so hard to become a proletarian; it is only a habit to be acquired: "After having turned the wheel for a few days, I felt that my body, once accustomed to this mechanical labor, could keep at it for a long time."[24] But this habit, which bends the body to the constraint of labor, also makes it incapable of *representing* transfiguration. Instead of the promised language and transfiguration, the apostle discovers the solitude of speechless labor: "I would wake up at four-thirty in the morning and go to bed at nine o'clock at night, often without having spoken to anyone; I did my work, I earned my salary, and I was content with myself."[25] The routine of proletarian existence reduces apostolic communion to the egotistical satisfaction of self-improvement, if not to simple material survival. The element of fire is only necessity, in which the financier kills the apostle: "Hoart had stripped the work of the proletariat of all poetry and saw things exclusively from the point of view of production: everyone, according to him, should turn the wheel because it paid forty sous a day."[26]

The men of circulation can then turn back to their advantage the canonical opposition of words and deeds: proletarian labor cannot double itself, cannot serve as a matter for its own representation. The new man cannot yet bloom in any industrial work; he can only announce himself in song and play. The work to come must recruit worker-poets, more sensitive to the voice, to the song and celebrations of the apostles, than to their silent labor. It is the artist, the proleptic union of contraries (water and fire, labor and voyage, masculine and feminine ...), who must resolve the contradiction inherent in the virile one-sidedness of industrial labor, prefigure the reign of the *Mother* who will poeticize the proletarian work [*œuvre*]. The impossible edification of the pacific army of laborers must be replaced by "the criss-crossing of France by mobile columns of workers and bands of singers, traversing the different work sites and constantly recruiting for both the workplace and the festival."[27]

A labor of artists, thus: an organized voyage, with its marches to a drumbeat, much more suitable than individual reeducation, which is subject to the hazard of employment, to attest the religious fraternity and strict discipline of the soldier-priests of the future; its obligatory scansions that form so many events: the arrival and departure of the apostles, announced by the rumor of the curious, magnified by the enthusiasm of sympathizers, sublimated by the calm courage they oppose to the cries and stones of fanatics; the meals in the inns where the crowd gathers to observe the missionaries and listen to their songs; sermons amplified by the silence of the night; but also all the incidents and encounters that form so many symbols: the wind that comes up just at the right time to fill the travelers' sails; the forced halt in the huts of the fishermen who, instead of leaving behind their nets, give them as covers to the apostles for whom they made beds of rushes. At every moment, the space of the voyage offers artists the possibility of a staging that gives new labor the *visibility* and *readability* that cannot be ensured in the space of the workshop. An exemplary testimony is given by the spectacle solemnly staged by Saint-Simonian tailors on the ridge overlooking Montereau. Led by a proletarian poet, they create a suit in which, for once, the labor of the tailors does not risk disappearing:

> On the site where Napoleon gave the last signs of his military power, we will labor; where he destroyed, we will produce. . . . Then my companions began to make the trousers and the red vest of Delas. The people who saw us came running from all parts of the city. . . . While they were watching my brothers work, I, who do not know how to sew, not wishing to leave any blank space, began to read, and the people listened religiously to Dessessart's profession of faith and the text Michel dedicated to Lyon.[28]

A scene visible from all sides; an evangelical symbol and a Napoleonic symbol; an end and a beginning; actors/laborers making for the poorest among them a suit that is still a symbol; a reciter whose speech accompanies the language of deeds.... To leave no space empty and no time dead: what cannot be acted out can always be said, what is not seen can always be recounted. The voyage, not industry, is where nothing is lost.

It is this principle of *saturation* that commands the unfolding of the mission of the East. The itinerary is ripe for it. All cultivated people of the time know that there are two

Frances: the "dark" France of the west and south, land of religious and *compagnonnique* fanaticism; and the enlightened France of the north and east. Captain Hoart first led the Saint-Simonian troops into the first of these Frances, perhaps with the secret intent of hardening them in the fire of persecution and using the facts to convince them of the superior efficiency of the Lyonnais work [*œuvre*] of production. The artists' mission sets off toward the northeast, an egalitarian troop that recognizes the musician Rogé only as an "eldest brother." This "mission of art" that "addresses women" must nonetheless join labor—salaried day labor— to speech and song. Labor corresponding to this feminine vocation ("the earth is the domain of the mother"), but also responding to the optimal requirements of visibility:

> We are in vast lands and work by the day. The June sun rises. Armed with picks and hoes, our troop opens the breach. At half past eight, our meal is brought to us in the fields; we eat canned cornmeal and bread and lard with our hands. With bent backs we bear the weight of the day. When the sun sets, our day is over and it is time to go home. Let order be established, COMPANIONS, at a marching pace; and on your shoulders, the arm of the producer, the arm of the future. And we traverse villages, astonished and moved, singing the coming of the MOTHER and the glory of the laborer.[29]

It is useless to ask what they dig or hoe, for the profit of what master or what culture. The prestige of armies is not made by the details of service but by parades. But it remains to be asked for whom this parade is held. No doubt the villagers, "astonished and moved" by the passage of the troop, come to appreciate their work: "Experienced old men said loudly that regular day laborers would do no more work than us and would not do it better." But it is obviously not this appreciation of ordinary capacity that can glorify the apostles. Or rather, if it does glorify them, this is done for others: those bourgeois who formerly laughed at the caricatures of the apostles of Ménilmontant as scullery boys and street sweepers:

> Haughty depreciators of our faith, come, come see doctors, lawyers, poets, musicians, mathematicians, men of the elite, men to whom the old society gave honor and consideration for their talents, bent over and working the earth with their hands. And this is no frivolous game, no amateur's amusement. . . . Ah! We now know what a rural proletarian's day is. Choirmasters of all parties who aspire to win the people's confidence, can you say as much?[30]

Beyond the people with whom one communes, the relation of visibility essentially establishes a connection between the voyagers playing soldier and keeping their logbook and the absent spectators to whom their narrative is addressed. The relation is all the more exemplary in the baptism by fire whereby the peasants' ill luck gives the apostles their chance: "One morning . . . , a companion sees far off, behind a forest, a wide column of smoke." Along with the fire of the forge and that of battle, the flames of conflagration play a well-determined role in the social and political imaginary of the time. They bring into light the obscure heroes of the laboring people who risk their lives to come to the rescue of others while people of position, titles, and honors keep a respectful distance from the danger. More than labor in the fields, the conflagration is the occasion when the companions can manifest their identity in the peasants' eyes: bourgeois who flee or men of the people who sacrifice themselves. Thus the troop strikes out immediately in the direction of the accident, seven miles away.

> We cross fields and woods where, for lack of an established path, we tore up our feet.... We reach a large pond barring our route, we cross it up to our chests in water.... Thirty houses were burning, we rush ahead. Here are the red berets! Here are the Saint-Simonians! Courage, courage! ... We are on the water line, at the pump, in the midst of the flames, everywhere. At one o'clock in the morning, we were still putting out the last embers.

Despite their exaltation, the narcissistic pleasure of the obstacle course and the heroic solidarity manifested with the villagers still count less than the symbol and lesson addressed to an absent third party:

> You who have spread and mongered so many lying accusations against us, you who accuse us of wanting to destroy property, come see us amidst the flames of Brazay, come see us defend property against conflagration and

save from fire goods that we respect because they are the fruit of men's labor. It is not with words but with acts that we answer you.[31]

Here is the true baptism by fire: not in the hardening of the young lovers of the people, but in the possibility of making a point of reality immediately correspond to every concept, an itinerary on a survey map correspond to every argument. If modern utopia has a meaning, it is assuredly not in the myth of the island that is nowhere, but, to the contrary, in this possibility of showing the adequation of text and reality at every point. Thus the apostles of utopia catch in reality's trap those realists of the *juste milieu* who reproach the apostles both for speaking of things that do not exist and for endangering property, the foundation of all social order. Now it is possible to show them in a single gesture that effective practice and property in its materiality are both on the side of the so-called anarchist dreamers: the houses in flames *are* the property defended by the Saint-Simonians, whereas that of the bourgeois speechifiers is only a *word*.

Between the speech of the doctrine and the deeds of the little band there is no blank space, no interstice by which doubt or refutation can slip in. This is the meaning of travel: to establish at each step, between the order of discourse and the order of facts, the immediate correspondence of the lines on the map and the undulations of the ground. The old correspondence of the microcosm and the macrocosm rises up again next to the science that supposedly had banished it. An immediate and perpetual transmutation of flesh and verb that makes every episode of the band's travel journal a message irrefutably inscribed in the landscape of social reality. *Come! Come see!* Everything is already contained in these imperatives, in the gesture that sets the troop in march and interpellates the witness, who of course will not come, but who, by not coming, shows himself as disqualified—just like he who does not voyage, who will never get down from his horse to pick the perilous flower of popular labor, dramas, and festivals: a magic flower that virtually inscribes tenderness for the daily life of the people in the universe of miracles. A miracle of water that follows upon the sacrifice of fire like the people's Sundays follow their weeks of labor:

> Sunday is here. . . . Dance, dance, good men and lovable women of the village! After having shared your fatigues, the COMPANIONS wish to share your pleasures. . . . And, far from breaking the fiddler's violin as the Christian priest would, it is under our fingers that the instrument of the dance will resonate. . . . In the middle of the ball, a circle of men and women forms. Our songs strike the air, we offer a word. While an attentive ear is lent to the orator, the clouds wandering in the atmosphere come together; a few drops of rain fall. Hooray! Hooray! For it has not rained for two months and the wheat is parched in the fields and the vegetables dying in the gardens! Earth and air commune in an abundant rain just as we commune with these good cultivators.[32]

A communion brought to term by earth and air, fire and water. But also a story definitively closed upon itself. The bourgeois cynics are no longer invited to attend: how could they fail to laugh at the tale of these sermons that bring rain? From this point on the apostles speak only to themselves. A voyage recited in advance, an anticipation of what has no meaning other than its being written in the *Livre des actes* published in Paris by Marie Talon? Who will read it? Father Enfantin and his companions, preparing the voyage to Egypt, who are already having the archives of the Doctrine copied? The other missionaries who are crisscrossing France? the tailor Delas, somewhere between Auch and Rodez (but it is not certain he knows how to read...)? the defrocked priest Terson, who has made himself a prisoner's suit in order to bear witness to the suffering of the disinherited in the far-off villages of the "desert" of the Landes, or among the colliers of the Ariège, who take him to be the Wandering Jew? the typesetter Biard, who has set out to "consecrate labor" in Angers and Nantes? the lawyer Duguet, who evangelizes the Massif Central? or rather those who have not left? the faithful workers who come together on Sunday at Ménilmontant or at the Barrière des Amandiers, caring little for the risks of travel but grateful toward those who travel to poeticize their existence? the bourgeois of the "Churches" of Bordeaux, Toulouse, Castelnaudary, or Castres... become reasonable once again but happy that others are unreasonable in their place and nostalgic for these stories that make an imperceptible difference in their ineluctable destiny as regional notables?...

Roads of the future, landscapes of nostalgia, recollections of vacation... the travelers will henceforth cross only their dream, already written somewhere: in the night of

Auxonne, where their religious songs fall "upon the enraptured people like the waves of a celestial harmony"; at Saint-Jean-de-Losne, which "prepared a temple for them, a roof of green chestnut trees lit up as if for a festival"; at Lons-le-Saunier strewn with the flowers of Corpus Christi, where, in the warmth of the evening, under a dais of greenery, they announce the coming of the Mother, making tears flow and hope shine in the eyes of women insatiable for new love: "The women, these women want to see us, hear us again. Groups form, conversations start up and the bowers of the garden ring with lively talk, with religious conferences in which the voice of *woman* rises up to equality with that of man . . . a whole city is born to the new life. The city saw us only one day and loved us as if she had seen us forever."[33]

Passing loves, supreme voluptuousness and mortal risk of a voyage already concluded but that can no longer stop. Nevertheless the Orient is already found: "The next day . . . we climbed the heights from which one can see the city nested in the depths of the valley. Farewell Lons-le-Saunier! Rest in peace on your slopes of green vines like a young sultana amidst cool pillows." But this is also what requires going further: "Farewell we leave you happy hopes and sweet premonitions of the future. A GIRL of the Orient will bring them to pass and your good wines will soon flow for the new nuptials."[34]

Nothing is more difficult than returning from a voyage where one always finds oneself at home. They will soon set sail for Egypt. There the sculptor Alric and the postmaster Maréchal, seeking the GIRL of the Orient, will die of the same plague as Captain Hoart, who had set off for the virile task of damming the river. The worker-poet Mercier will be more prudent. He will be content to return to Paris and throw himself into the Seine.

Punishment for their presumptuousness. They had claimed to walk far from the beaten paths of politics. They did not know that, among all the futilities that it teaches and puts to work, there is one truly indispensable science: that of ending a journey.

Their nephews will be better prepared.

The People's Song

Return to reason? What reason? Doubtless we should ask this German student who, on a May day in Strasbourg, met a wanderer from the mission of the East, the apostle Rousseau, who has volunteered to go share the fate of Siberian prisoners, but has already been refused passage at Augsburg.

> If the other day the clear skies had allowed you to see all the way to the cathedral, you would have found me sitting next to a bearded young man with long hair. He had a red beret on his head, a cashmere scarf around his neck, a short German jacket on his carcass, the name Rousseau sewn on his vest, tight trousers with stirrups on his legs, and a fashionable little cane in his hand. As you can see, the caricature is put together from several centuries and continents: Asia around the neck, Germany on the body, France on the legs, 1400 on the head, and 1833 in his hand. And he is a cosmopolitan—no, more than that, he is a Saint-Simonian! . . . Rousseau and his traveling com-

panion (neither of whom understand a word of German) have come to Germany to seek the femme, but they were turned back at the border: an intolerable stupidity. I told him that he had not lost much in women but that women had lost much in him.... He is now staying in Strasbourg, keeping his hands in his pockets and preaching labor to the people, is compensated according to his capacity and marche vers les femmes, as he puts it. He is moreover entirely to be envied and leads the most comfortable life under the sun, and, purely out of laziness, I would like to become a Saint-Simonian so that I too would be remunerated according to my true capacity.[35]

The student, Büchner, has three reasons to mock the companion of the Woman. Firstly, he is studying medicine, the nervous system in particular, and his scientific gaze is merciless toward the mystical utopia of the new love. Secondly, this young man, not well disposed toward a revolution in morals, is writing to his parents and, in this circumstance, he prefers to adopt a detached tone when speaking of political troubles and intellectual subversions—because, and this is the essential point, this student is a revolutionary. Were he to return to see the countryside of his own land, it would not be to play the fiddle or paint landscapes, but to bear the incendiary message that could set the peasants off to assault the manors where the lords live off the sweat of the poor.

Scientific materialism, revolution of the popular masses. Where the solipsistic vagabondage of the lovers of the people ran into the barrier of the repressive state is where

THE NEW LAND   43

the royal road to knowledge of revolutionary action should begin.

The thing begins with what is said to be the principle of modern science: measurable quantity, the laws of motion, the calculus of forces. "If a revolution is ever to be successful, it can and must come solely from the masses, who will crush the soldiers by weight of their numerical superiority." The problem is to set the masses in motion. But, "in all impartiality," one must admit that the people "have a relatively primitive outlook, and sad to say, they are only accessible through their purse." Sad, but practical: it is enough to do the accounting, to show them in black and white "that they belong to a state which they support in great measure while others benefit from them, that most of the taxes are drawn from their property—hard to maintain in any case—while the capitalists go scot-free."[36]

This is the statistical program of the *Hessian Messenger*, establishing that of the 6,363,436 guldens paid by the 718,373 inhabitants of the Grand Duchy of Hesse, 1,551,502 go to paying the tax collectors who organize this robbing of the people, 1,110,607 to the judges and policemen who oblige the people by force to respect it, 914,820 to the soldiers who crack the skulls of those who protest, and so on, down to the very last gulden. This breakdown provides an exact verification of what, elsewhere, will be expressed in antithetical images borrowed from the prose of *L'Ami du peuple*: that the princes, aristocrats, and their wives have dyed their gowns in the people's sweat, cut their ribbons from the calluses of the people's hands, built their palaces with the people's bones, and even concocted their makeup from the tears of widows and orphans.

Such, with the addition of a few biblical verses due to the inspiration of Pastor Weidig, is the demonstration that a few accomplices will slip under a few peasants' doors in July 1834. And here begin the disappointments of revolutionary science. The statistics that the young student carefully annotated for the *Hessian Messenger* will prove nothing to the Grand Duchy's peasants, except perhaps that the whole thing reeked of heresy and that it was better to call the police yourself than to wait for them to come knocking. His companions locked up while the noose was tightening around him, the young man will head back to Strasbourg in the spring of 1835, more discreetly but just as quickly as the apostle Rousseau.

This short voyage of science was apparently just as fruitless as the utopian peregrinations of the apostles of the new love. For winning over the people, would figures be every bit as vain as the refrains of love? Perhaps this is too mechanical, too arithmetical a conception of science? Or would the error rather lie in wanting to insert the incalculable element of consciousness between the figures of oppression and the force of armies? In either case we would be forced to come to the same conclusion. Henceforth the young man will stick to the teachings of the natural sciences.

A first divorce between science and the revolution. This does not mean that the revolution has been superseded or impugned by science. What is left behind is the idea that science can do anything for the revolution. "The relationship between the poor and the rich is the only revolutionary element in the world": the relationship, not the knowledge [*science*] and consciousness [*conscience*] of the relation, which is the usual object of these voyages into the heart of the people, either seeking the materials of science or bringing the weapons of consciousness.[37] What is impugned by the science of nature and the experience of politics are the two happy figures of the revolution informed by reason: the world governed by *mathesis*, society regulated by the communication of rational thought. The operation of science is not a calculus of number and figure that could organize a world subject to rational mastery and a community of reason. It is a dissection that never reaches its end, that never reaches the point from which an inverse movement could begin, the happy communication of knowledge and love uniting material atoms and sensitive fibers.

This is the message of the theatrical parable whose pages the young man, working under the double surveillance of police and family, hides under his anatomical engravings. The opening lines of *Danton's Death* give a scientific explanation of why the action is already at its end and the revolution of enlightenment impossible: for its promise to be kept would require the same thing that every oath of love lacks, namely a connection between two brains that could be formed only by smashing both skulls open and linking together, one by one, the fibers of each brain.[38]

The new promise of happiness could be kept only if the work of dissection, the infinite regress of science, were able to come to an end. The first scene of each act, each false promise of action, will renew the demonstration. It would only be worth fighting against the terrorist revolution if the enlightened revolution were possible. Science would have to be able finally to find this thing that is lacking, for which we have no name since it is nothing but the fault in creation.[39] The labor of science is infinite division, the same as the counting of days, the same as the labor of nature which is only the interminable wound of creation, of the mishap or first error that sculpted the creature's pain out of nothingness. If rational science can do nothing for the revolution, it is not because it would dissipate the soft clouds of its sunlit dreams; on the contrary, it does the same labor of the same bad dream. Science and revolution are condemned to do, in solitude, the same thing. The revolution too is a never-finished, infinite division, condemned to sophism and dissection. It is the mourning of the happy ideal of mathematics, making its actors into "mathematicians of the flesh, [who] in [their] hunt for the ever elusive $x \ldots$, write their equations with the bleeding fragments of human limbs."[40]

Never will reason be able to represent itself as the communicable project of a common moral enterprise. The terror bears witness to the fact that thought only ever acts as blindly as nature. It only becomes action as hallucination, word become flesh, rhetoric that carves living flesh. This is why it is vain to expect the revolution to come from the teaching of the people by its cultivated visitors. If there is anything other than hunger that can put the masses in motion, it is the fanaticism of the crucified word. "Our age needs weapons and bread—and then a *cross* or some such."[41] There is nothing that the educated class can do for the revolution, only against it: "only a new Moses inflicting the Seven Plagues of Egypt upon us could be our Messiah. Fatten the peasants, and the revolution will die of apoplexy."[42] The revolution is a catastrophe within the catastrophe of nature. Like nature the revolution sculpts into the flesh, it destroys this wound in the nothingness that is the proliferating creation that has overtaken everything. The revolution will never be done with killing, just as science will never be done with knowing.

This is the illusion of the repentant and the disillusioned. The revolution is not over. It has the future on its side, nature's future: to destroy the wound of creation. And it would be just as foolish to believe in an equitable partition of heaven and earth, in the reasonable separation of the clouds of summer and the troubles of society. The poetic critique of voyages to the land of the revolution needs to go a step further and recognize that the same verbal hallucination links the clouds of the sky of poetry and the storms of the revolution. There are not two different regimes of sentences. The sentence always carves into the flesh. There is no salvation promised for merely recognizing the original sin that stays short of all the ills that the sword seeks to cure. In vain does the sinner, Woyzeck's adulterous companion, kneel while invoking the son of man. As the executioner Robespierre put it, the son of man is crucified in all of us. There is no savior for those who repent because the evil is not in the creature but in creation. There is no witness to evil, no voice for the abandoned child. The child is abandoned short of any sin and any redemption. This is what the grandmother who tries to distract the children in Marie's place recounts in a radically altered version of a Grimm's fairy tale:

> Once upon a time there was a poor child, had no father and no mother, everyone was dead and there was nobody left in all the world. Everyone dead, and the child went and cried both day and night. And seeing there was nobody left on earth, he wanted to go up to heaven, and the moon gave him such a friendly look, and when in the end he came to the moon, it was a lump of rotten wood, so he went to the sun, and when he came to the sun, it was a withered sunflower, and when he came to the stars, they where tiny golden insects stuck there as though by a butcher-bird on blackthorn, and when he wanted to come back to earth again, the earth was an upturned cookpot, and he was all alone, so he sat down and cried, and he's sitting there still, all alone on his own.[43]

No journey's end can be described as the enthusiasts' return to earth. The lovers of daffodils end up with an upside-down flower pot. It would take some strange children to listen to such a tale, such as the ones who will happily look at Marie's massacred body. But perhaps things should be turned around and we should say that such things can only be said as a joke, or to children, or in a fiction in which the great historical drama of the terror, the ordinary crime of a soldier like Woyzeck and the burlesque wedding of Prince Leonce are on the same level.

After all, even scandal has limits, a form of decency. The century will only accept two of them, which eventually will sum it up: utopia and science. There is the scandal figured by the improbable getup of the apostle Rousseau: the utopia of new love, sanctified labor, the free woman, and the light in the east. And there is the scandal that in another twenty years will be borne by Ludwig Büchner, the little brother who for the moment is still playing children's games: scientific materialism, which knows neither beginning nor end to the world, nothing but the eternity of force and motion; which grants the soul no properties other than those of the brain and grants man no superiority over the beasts other than having reached a further stage of evolution. Intolerable words that nonetheless announce a beautiful and reasonable future to humanity: advancement toward superior forms of life, the end of superstition and abject poverty, the progress of science and democracy, the association of capital and labor, the triumphal route that, having led from ape to man, will lead from barbarism to the rule of reason.

Even if they pay the price—a few stones thrown at them, a period of destitution—Achille Rousseau and Ludwig Büchner will still have chosen the easier path, that of the scandal that leads to the progress of enlightenment, morals, and governments. What remains for Georg Büchner is something that cannot be heard, something that exceeds the double scandal of science and utopia: the knowledge of their identity, the knowledge that revolutions are just as reasonable and mad, just as aleatory and ineluctable, as earthquakes or hurricanes; the dark side of the triumphant future, the deadly secret that shadows the marriage of science and revolution, the secret that cannot be thought but only notched in the flesh, in millions of wounded bodies. It can be said at least in a fable like *Danton's Death*, dashed off in five weeks, as if he had to hurry not only on account of the police keeping watch outside the family home, but also on account of little Ludwig playing a few feet away.

But perhaps that's a little too pathetic. A play is only a play. And it's a way to make a little money, which will come in handy when it comes time to live abroad. Perhaps we need to recall, in opposition to the melancholy of Prince Leonce, who flees an arranged marriage and the propagation of the species, the wisdom of the clown Valerio. In the play of summer clouds at sunset, the prince sees menacing specters covering the earth, curled up like a baby in its cradle. But in the eyes of the clown the red blood of the setting sun and the wounded world is only the sign of the inn The Golden Sun.[44] The infinity of empty time and interminable dissection can also be experienced as the game of science serving to kill time: the carp and frogs the student dissects to improve his knowledge of the nervous system and get his doctorate; the future as a scientist and philosopher that is open to the young doctor in Switzerland, land of exile for revolutionaries—but also the land of fattened peasants, where the revolution is superfluous, as the new assistant professor boasts to his nervous parents:

> All along the way, friendly villages with pretty houses, and then the nearer you get to Zurich, and especially along the lake, prosperity on every hand. . . . The streets here aren't

full of soldiers, aspiring civil servants and idle state officials, and you don't run the risk of being knocked down by an aristocrat's carriage; instead of that, everywhere you see a healthy, vigorous people, governed at little cost by a simple, good, truly republican government.[45]

But the scientist's scalpel is no different than the worker's tool. Once you get used to it, plenty of time—too much time—is left for poetic reverie. And not that much time is needed to discover what happy people lack, something unknown in Strasbourg or Darmstadt: they have forgotten how to sing. Whence the young assistant professor's appeal to his fiancée who is supposed to come visit him from Strasbourg for Easter in 1837: "Could you learn those *folksongs* by Eastertime if it wouldn't be too much to ask of your health. One doesn't hear any singing here; the *people* don't sing."[46]

A rather strange insistence, to demand as the proof of a woman's love the performance of popular songs…. Could it be a late nostalgia for the "Woman" he once mocked, who was supposed to guide the apostles on their voyages into the heart of the true people? At about the same time, the apostle Rousseau publishes a work called *La Magdeleine*. Rousseau preaches the virtues of labor in two volumes of poetic prose that show Mary of Magdala corrupted by the idleness and luxuriousness of her family, debauching herself all the way from the banks of the Nile to the banks of the Eurotas. For the love of this courtesan, the rich son of a Roman senator, a poet, throws the most exorbitant of parties. But the musician he has summoned from Athens has traveled too little or too badly to make worthwhile music from his voyages. And Mary Magdalene's lover reproaches him for it bitterly:

> "You have passed through the world without the world being reflected in you, without allowing the world to be printed in living characters. There has been written in you nothing of the drama, of the dream, of the labor, or of the celebration of life. Neither earth nor sky; neither seas nor mysterious and ancient vapors; neither imperial triumph nor village wedding . . . , not the thousands upon thousands of crafts of the hard-working people, not the thousands upon thousands of rites and celebrations of the diverse peoples of the earth, not the thousands upon thousands of joys and the thousands upon thousands of sorrows that make their hearts beat. . . . So you are incapable of making the music I ask for. . . . We will have to be content with the simple and naive songs that the people of every nation sing in their sorrow and joy, in war and celebration, without ever knowing where and they learned them.
>
> "My beloved knows a few of these songs."[47]

An imaginary ethnomusicology, worthy of this traveler who can talk endlessly about bitter returns from excursions never taken. Could Doctor Büchner ever listen, without laughing, to such a presentation of the great love of the people, as if it were a coin collection of popular songs, arts, and traditions? In any case he is lucky enough to already have the *Knaben Wunderhorn* at his disposal, so he can count out for the Saint-Simonian apostle every one of the thousands upon thousands of crafts, thousands upon thousands of joys, thousands upon thousands of sorrows. The scalpel teaches us more about popular song with a single stroke than all these fantastical myriads, and while Achille Rousseau was going on and on about the sources of the Ganges and the ruins of Palmyra, his old interlocutor was trying to decipher the gazes of children he encountered in the festivals and fairs of Alsace. "I have just come from the Christchild fair, everywhere there were swarms of ragged, freezing children who stand with wide-open eyes and mournful faces in front of these splendors made from water and flour, crap and gilded paper."[48]

If we could only know how these dreams and resentments will come of age ... Will it be in the feverish and indifferent desires of plebeian Magdalenas? Marion, she of the insatiable desires and embraces, who sees no difference between the pleasure of holy images and that of lovers' bodies? Marie, she who doesn't seem to care about anything, except perhaps the handsome uniform of a drum major, or the shine of earrings in a piece of broken mirror? Or in the fears and superstitions of a soldier like Woyzeck, struggling with "second nature," the underground noises that may come from the freemasons, the figures on the ground where the mushrooms grow, and the world that seems to go up in flames? In the tales told by idiots, grandmothers' stories, the patter of carnival barkers, the whining of a hurdy-gurdy, and the amusements of craftsmen who "piss on the cross that a Jew might die"? An enigma—which does not speak to the workers of the revolution or the vacationers of love—of the "true" people, who have just as much reason to submit as to revolt, who have as much at stake in revolution and counterrevolution. A privileged object of study for those in search of reasons to despair, but also for those who seek the means to make the people rise up.

As it happens, it is neither one nor the other: neither the second return of the disabused nor the curved path of the strategists. Both of these presume that science has a power capable of mastering the people's obscure superstitions. But science is only one way to kill time, and Woyzeck's madness is also the result of his learned major's experiment. The popular choruses of *Woyzeck* accompany the descent into the abysses that surround the land of prosperity and those that undermine science's seat: a voyage that gives no privilege, undertaken by one who has lived through the initial divorce of the paths of consciousness and those of the revolution, who has learned that history's reason is strictly identical to its madness: "I feel ever closer to the people and to the Middle Ages, it seems clearer to me every day."[49]

Where would he have come to if typhoid fever had allowed him to age beyond his twenty-fourth year? Perhaps it would be better to stay with the wise unreason of the apostle Rousseau, whose Magdalena, once the orgy was over, heard the voice calling her toward the worker from Nazareth and his cross, the beginning of a world of labor and of love. Once he had gone back to his Angevin homeland, his main concern was to instruct the peasant masses by the example of modern agriculture and the practice of choral song. The former companion of the Woman found his Ludwig in the person of Eugène Bonnemère, the young editor of the *Précurseur de l'ouest*, who explores, on behalf of progress, the land of "pious beliefs," of "primitive faith" and "proverbial naivete."[50] And he would later give his seventeen thousand pages of manuscripts to one who would write, in a great democratic salute to the young Third Republic, the *Histoire des paysans français*.

But this does not mean that he stayed closed up in his model farm. It is said that he went from town to town to give the people musical education, and even that he went all the way to Switzerland to find the right voices for singing his free songs.

He will have been distinctly more happy than the young skeptic he met in Strasbourg. It is nice to imagine him in the Zurich cemetery, meditating before the two verses by Herwegh that decorate Georg Büchner's grave:

Ein unvollendet Leid sinkt er ins Grab
Der verse schönsten nimmt er mit hinab.

An unfinished song lies in this grave
He has taken with him his most beautiful verses.

But it is doubtful that he ever learned German.

The Mirror of the Sea

One missed rendezvous can always hide another. No doubt the apostles were something less than reasonable. But perhaps the one they sought was not where he belonged, sent far off by some secret madness. In any case, at the same time that the Saint-Simonian missionaries were heading deeper into the Orient of labor and of the Mother, the proletarian Claude Genoux was hunting for the white whale around Cape Horn.

Another voyage, however, which looks like neither a flight nor a quest. Not everyone can be called Ishmael. There seems nothing biblical or metaphysical in the adventures of Claude Genoux, from Cape Horn to the Bering Strait. Whatever sent him to the ends of the world was neither the destitution of the well-born person who has fallen on hard times, nor the seduction of the Leviathan, nor even Narcissus's fascination with the mirror of the ocean.

What was it then? Somewhere in Brazil, a slave, the former king of an African tribe, posed the question to him. Was he not there, like all white men, to exploit the subject populations? No, answered the voyager, "I came here as I have been elsewhere. I seek to live, to learn, and I find my happiness in roaming all around the wide world."[51]

Of course he was lying a little. In fact it was business that made the young man leave Marseilles, where he split his time between carrying bricks for masons, cleaning boots, and writing complaints for peddlers and mystery plays for village festivals.

> One day when returning from the work site, eating a bit of bread for supper, I found in the alleys of Meilhan an unsealed letter, written by a trader in Rio de Janeiro. The postscript of the letter said something along these lines: "a particularly important item would be leeches; if you can send me twenty thousand by July, I can promise to sell them for three hundred reis apiece."
>
> "Three hundred reis per leech!" I cried with astonishment; three hundred reis!!! I have no idea what the value of a reis is, but what difference does it make; if it's a good deal for someone else it's a good deal for me.[52]

No sooner said than done: the young man convinced two Piedmontese, who sold strings for musical instruments and shared his lodgings, to join him. They bought three wine barrels, cut them in half, and lined them with lead. This allowed them to "comfortably" take ten thousand leeches to Rio. Lucky enough to sell his merchandise when he landed, the Savoyard got rid of his two partners, thanks to the benevolent help of a shark and an alligator, and became the sole beneficiary of the profits of the deal.

So now he travels around Brazil peddling music boxes and various knickknackery. Now he's a businessman. *Him* or *someone else, here* or *there*, just like the commodity that has no homeland and the gold that makes everything equivalent. But might not the mistake be to want always to separate things: wandering and business, tourism and work, school and life? Has Claude Genoux ever done anything else but live this confusion of opposites, ever since the childhood he spent in the company of adults, chimneysweeps or traveling salesmen, wandering across the farms, fairs, and markets of Bresse, sharing the fate of boys destined, according to their strength, to haul merchandise, sweep chimneys, or beg? Since he sneaked away from the troop near Chalon, he has been an acrobat in Auxerre, a chimneysweep in Joigny, an inmate in the Foundling Hospital in Paris, a domestic servant in Romorantin, a thirteen-year-old tourist in Rome, a deckhand in the Sardinian navy, a shepherd in the countryside, a reseller of theater tickets in Paris again, an army cook during the Algerian campaign.... An adventurous existence, but the adventure always becomes banal in its forms and optimized in its results. In one way or another, everything is made profitable: the complaints for which he charges three francs regardless of length (or quality); the mystery plays paid in ticket receipts; but also the imprisonment in the Foundling Hospital, which pays in the sense that it enables him to learn to read; domestic servitude compensated for by the master's library rather than the gild of the livery; or the job of cleaning boots, paid *a contrario* in self-esteem. A logic of accumulation, in which profits in gold, education, and enjoyment are added and equated in a single account book: "At the age of eighteen, I had seen all of the old world; I had given myself the bit of education that I possess; and the best deal of all was that, by virtue of setting aside an apple in case you get thirsty, as they say in my country, I had managed to sew a thousand francs worth of gold coins into my belt."[53]

A way of making wandering profitable. But also risks that are necessary if he wants to realize the far-off dream of the little chalet and retirement in his homeland. A thousand gold coins won't get it done, and this is why the poet-bootblack was in Marseilles waiting for the chance at a fortune that it was entirely logical to seek on the continent he did not yet know.

So he set sail for Rio with his leeches and other merchandise that he had smuggled aboard. This other merchandise was what led to all the rest. Unable to sell it in the capital, Genoux was obliged to prolong his journey. He went inland to try to peddle it, crossing mountains, floods, and forests; reinvested the profits from his sales in a partnership with a Milanese; got rid of this crooked partner during a shipwreck, in which their fortune went down too; wound up landing on Robinson's old island, which had become a Chilean penal colony; took part in an armed insurrection in Peru; became a cook on an American whaler in the Arctic Circle and then a whale hunter himself on a French whaler in the South Seas.... And every step of this drifting is carefully calculated: three young girls met at the fountain on the island of Juan Fernandez; a peak a hundred meters high, climbed to enjoy an immense panorama overlooking the Pacific and the cordillera of the Andes (howeverimmense, it can still be figured as fifty leagues filled with twenty small islands); ten gourdes to be won in Valparaiso in order to pay for his wedding with a fiancée who meanwhile died from leprosy; four whale boats and twenty-four oarsmen beating the waves to kill a whale, whose blood spurted fifteen to twenty feet into the air; five inches of snow covering a hillside from which the traveler can contemplate the landscape of Kamchatka in the boreal night, temperature fifteen degrees Réaumur; four huge black dogs hauling an indigenous funeral train to the top of that same hill; four cakes shared by the wandering sailor as a funeral meal; four kilometers in five minutes of vertiginous descent, chasing after the dogs who had got loose and run off three minutes earlier; the yurt covering a hundred square meters, where his companions lead him, a "phalanstery" where the soot hangs in black stalactites and the flesh of grilled bears, otters, and fish are mixed with the breath of a multitude of men, women, children, foxes, and dogs; eighteen Polynesian pirogues pulling up alongside the ship to propose the unacceptable barter of a load of coconuts for the galley's cooking equipment; the accepted barter of this "French" sailor picked up by an American whaler for an American sailor picked up by a French whaler; four hundred sixty-seven francs brought back to Granville as the wages of these four years of peregrinations and reduced overnight to thirteen francs by the obligation to buy a farewell round....

Genoux's voyage is constantly governed by the law of equivalencies and compensations: love found at the price of cargo lost, on this island populated by convicts who turn out to be the most honest men in the world; the beloved lost, attacked by a leper, while her fiance is off enjoying the unforgettable view... That is, if one lends credence to this love story that begins on the banks of a stream, where the fresh young maidens welcoming the shipwrecked sailor look a little too much like Nausicaa's companions.... But why should we be more suspicious of this story than that of the unsealed letter in Marseilles or the providential shark and alligator? Isn't the logic of travel also to be found in this equivalence of what is *seen* and what is *read*, of the true and the false, of morality and cynicism? And wasn't all this already said in the preface to the Savoyard's *Mémoires*, linking the traveler's fate to that of the book? There we were told how, at the age of sixteen, the former chimneysweep, having set off for Marseilles to seek his fortune in the South Seas, and having embarked at Lyon on a coal barge going down the Rhône, was forced to spend a night on an island in the middle of the river. "There," he tells us,

> in a poor hut where the boatmen gave me hospitality, I found on a plank a book half devoured by worms; this book, which no longer had a title, seemed to contain the adventures and first poetical stirrings of a young man named Leonard. I spent a wonderful night reading this book, full of great deeds and adventures. In the morning, when it was time to go and leave behind this volume that did not belong to me and that these good folk would not give me because it constituted their entire library all by itself, I felt as if I were saying good-bye forever to a dear

friend. . . . Fifteen years have passed since that day; fifteen years during which I have traveled around the world without ever having found a single copy of this work of poetry, in France or elsewhere; without ever having found anyone who could tell me about it. I think that I can therefore call myself the only man alive today who knows of its existence. Indeed! Far from the oblivion in which this book has fallen having discouraged me, it has in fact given me the force and will to write the present book in the same genre.[54]

Let's not worry about the "studious young man" who might in turn find this new book in some smoke-filled cabin. Nor about the nowhere-to-be-found Leonard. What we should notice here is that, from the island in the Rhône to that of Robinson Crusoe, the traveler has never left the island of the book. He is the only one who knows of the existence of the book, who knows whether it is true or false that it ever existed. He is also the only one to know whether or not he himself landed on Robinson's island, the island of the exemplary worker that is also the most perfect creation of the imagination: the unique book of poor children but also the only one Rousseau gives to Emile: the book of the island that teaches the child all the virtues of human striving and all the illusory delights of the imaginary.

Can the morality of the traveler also be that of the worker? This is the question that haunts the review of the work appearing in *L'Atelier*, organ of the moral and material interests of the workers, even as the proper doses of praise and blame to be bestowed on the Savoyard get a little confused. The reviewer gives high praise to the moral demonstration of the virtues of effort and perseverance in confronting and overcoming adversity. And the few bodies that must be lightly tossed overboard for this end do not much embarrass his conscience as a Christian and a man of progress. He particularly appreciates the brutal conclusion, where the author recommends the use of forced labor to reeducate the good-for-nothings of the species and the poets who claim to be unable to find their place in society. But the story would be better, the reviewer thinks, "if the hero went on a little less about his poetical impressions (impressions that all vulgar tourists feel) and gave a little more care to recounting all the details and sufferings of this life as a vagabond." Thus more realism, but not the sort of realism he picked up in *Gil Blas*, for example: "if a few of the amorous adventures that are told a little too freely and that the reader might mistake for chapters in a novel, were instead softened or simply suppressed, the book would not suffer at all. It seems to us to have been at best useless to put into action the song by Béranger that draws a parallel between a whore and a nun and awards equal merit to both."[55]

This is the sort of morality of travel that can be imagined by a Christian and socialist worker in Paris: one without a poet's landscape or a sinner's temptation. But the cynical Savoyard no doubt understands the religion of labor better than his reviewer does. Perhaps the liberties of this poet and adventurer were exactly what the practical demonstration of the morality put forth by the workers' newspaper needed: a morality of obligatory and accepted effort that makes all situations equivalent and gives all forms of labor an equal dignity. How could the chaste and sedentary editors understand the final lesson of the voyage: that the noble abstraction of duty is perhaps identical to the natural law of a world in which everything can be counted, bartered, substituted: men's labor, women's love, the truth and falsehood of stories? The poet's liberties, like the final pirouette that will send him back from the pen to the shovel, establish this endless reversibility between the morality of work and the immorality of life.

He must have been thinking about something like this when he watched the albatrosses frolicking about the dead whale. He did not admire them freely slicing through the skies of the ideal; he did not lament them limping clumsily on reality's floorboards. Under the poetical glimmering of moonbeams and the torchlight from the boats, he saw them unite the aerial perfection of flight with a quite earthly sense of reality, fighting the sailors for the pieces of the whale's carcass right up until it is cast off for them to share with the condors. And perhaps he was also thinking of this when they put into port in Chile and the sailors relaxed from the heroism of whaling by watching the fandango:

> There is nothing more indecent than this dance, particularly when, face-to-face, the caballero, enveloped in his wide poncho, wearing the high Guayaquil sombrero, makes lascivious gestures to the woman with each step he takes, and she responds with even more lascivious ones. Forty thousand leagues away from our mountains, seeing things that were so new for me, I thought of the chaste dances I saw every Sunday of my childhood on the village

commons. What a difference! But at the age of twenty-two, and particularly for a whaling man, it would have been ridiculous to lower my eyes, which I did not do. I turned back toward the table, and, after a free-for-all when our sailors danced a French contredanse with one another, I entered into the same delirium as our sailors whom I used to call wild beasts because, having never known pain, I could not feel pleasure; because, never having been bored, I did not know how to hold boredom at bay.[56]

"Things so new . . . I did not know . . . " : the peddler whose mechanical organs played Meyerbeer and Rossini on Brazilian *fazendas*, the adventurer who rediscovered Nausicaa on Robinson Crusoe's island and the phalanstery on Kamchatka deserved to find something new, at last, at the end of his odyssey. In fact, what he found was the boredom, the suffering and joy, the labor without poetry and the pleasures without refinement that the happenstance and wanderings of proletarian existences always come back to and always seek to escape. At the end of these adventures marked by the law of equivalences—a law of poetry, tourism, and commodities—he has recognized the foundation of universal equivalence: enclosure within the circle of the brutal efforts and pleasures of voiceless labor. A proletarian's hell that he seeks to flee all the way to the end of the world, where he finds it again exemplified in the figure of the free sailor on the high seas and the adventurous whale hunter.

A proletarian's face-off with himself. From the leeches to the whale, the wanderings of the commodity to the nudity of the proletariat, the indifference of the adventurer to Narcissus's mirror. It is not so easy to escape from metaphysics, from the dereliction of fallen children, or from the destiny of those who have imprudently linked the mirages of poetry with the positive realities of whale hunting. One succumbs on account of being recognized merely as a reporter of savage customs and maritime life. Another feigns in vain to renounce the pretensions of adventurers and poets. Claude Genoux can always conclude by honoring those who wield pickaxes. If he writes, he does so to pass from one condition to another, from someone who loads the paper to someone who lays out the pages, even someone who writes them. And he will not stop writing. Just as he will refuse to die in a bed in the hospice for aged workmen. Forty years after his return from the South Seas, the Savoyard, once again a bootblack by trade, will take off for a walk in the forest of Fontainebleau. Which is where, a few days later, his body will be found.

The Poor Woman

The Petrified Flower

After the meetings come letters. And, no doubt, we could say that there are true and false letters: those written by travelers and lovers and those published by pedagogues. Things get a little more complicated, though, when pedagogues talk about love and introduce us to travel through different ages and conditions.

To begin, then, a false letter: in 1962 Paul Viallaneix published Michelet's *Journal*, and in place of a preface he addresses his author in order to speak, a bit maliciously, about his difficult relations with women: the long martyrdom with Pauline, the false housewife; the brief paradise with Mme Dumesnil, the angel met at the graveside; the domestic and clandestine love affairs with the servants Marie and Victoire, rebaptized Barbara and Rustica. So speaks the commentator:

> The loss of Madame Dumesnil reawakens in you a veritable "desire for living reality." Marie and Victoire, servants with the freshness of the countryside, help you

assuage it. And gradually you come to take these love affairs on the side more and more seriously. You try to raise Marie, "Barbara," to your own level. You teach her the rudiments of writing, and eventually she learns to sign her name! Victoire, "Rustica," who is not illiterate, gives you more serious hopes. You guide her reading. You comment the stories of Ruth and Samson for her. Why shouldn't the people's historian marry a daughter of the fields? Alas, the intellectual progress of "Rustica" stalls. You abandon your dreams of being both lover and pedagogue, and retrospectively doubt the sincerity of those dreams....

At least one conviction can be drawn from your unhappy experiences: without a woman, no salvation.[1]

The letter—the false letter—is written in the tone of knowing impertinence specific to a pedagogue aware that he is addressing a century of freer morals, rarer domestic servitude, and more sophisticated ideas about both women and the people. Still, speaking elsewhere in the third person of the biographer, impertinence cedes its place to a positive rationalization of Michelet's "populism." In *La Voie royale*, Paul Viallaneix presents us with a long demonstration of this affirmation: Michelet is of the people, he comes from the people, and still behaves like one of the people. In his relations with women, in particular, he has the pragmatic attitude of a man of the people, governed by a dual sense of domestic economy and sexual hygiene. The first concern motivated his marriage with Pauline Rousseau, which he presented to his aunts as an excellent way for a young professor to reduce his laundry and food expenses. It was the second concern that, after the deaths of Pauline and Mme Dumesnil, led the Collège de France professor to separate spiritual fulfillment from the needs of the body. The inconsolable lover arrived at this division of things during a trip to Germany: "At first, along the dusty road, I drew sustenance from the impossible past. Then the desire for living realities, almost equally impossible, came to me and grew within me. Now it is time to pacify this desire in the prose that awaits me and to reinstate the old division: here, the body; there, for books and for the world, the heart."[2]

Thus the academic who is still a son of the people can be seen arranging for double service at home, thanks to his servants, keeping his heart free for books and the world. But this division is almost immediately disturbed; its pragmatism falls apart. Barbara and Rustica do more than assure the material comforts of the household and the body: they become initiators. They reveal to the conquering historian how much he does not know about his subject. They reveal to him precisely the rustic, barbarian origin of the French nation, the inexhaustible reserve of meaning of this origin, unknown by the literate classes who see medieval France as having been made by its kings and monks. Later, he will evoke this great division in his work in the fall of 1842 as "the heroic appearance of the people, as early as the fifth century, before the kings, before the monks, before all those who have been considered as the creators of the modern world."[3] This appearance was possible because the lover of Marie-Barbara was able to "immolate" in himself the man of letters and sit down beside the old source, "the profound inner point where instinct unites all life, natural, animal, human," where he could rediscover the "childlike, humble, innocent soul of the people."[4] That winter, he led his listeners through a course on the *rustici*, on the very meaning of *rusticus* and the rustic nature of those who made France: Saint Genêt the peasant, Saint Éloi the worker; he followed the oxen behind the plow. Lower still, he "picked out in the serf's hut the lowliest members of the family, the child and the animal."[5] Day by day, a whole series of equivalences—some modest, others scabrous—identify the return to the far-off historical source with the nearby satisfactions provided by the relationship with his serving woman. Thus, on January 20, 1843: "I have gotten back into my subject this morning, where I feel stronger and stronger. I feel ever more interest for the *rustici* of the fifth century."[6]

In the place where we should find the "populist" division of the body and the heart there is instead an affirmation of the call to union. The project of saving the heart for books and the world turns out to be nonsense. The world is cold, as are books, if they do not rest upon the unity of the body and the heart. The acquiescent body of the rustic or barbarian is also the subject of history deciphered, the recovered heart of the simple folk that revolutionizes the book. The same *subject* satisfies the man's desire and the requirements of the new science. But this unity cannot reside only in the book. The circle must be completed, the historian must give back to the people what the people have given to the book, the lover of the woman of the people must in turn initiate her who initiated him. This completed union of speech and flesh, this reciprocity of initiation is what is called democracy. Thus the historian began to "link together his life and his work," to find "the union of his acts and opinions": "love, education, democracy, in a word, initiation, mean to make their object higher, greater and more beautiful, to bring it to a higher degree of life . . . so that the person should grow, not in dependence and to our advantage, but in herself and in her own originality."[7]

Such is the pedagogical duty that makes the historian, the son of the people, read the story of Ruth the foreigner to the daughter of the fields. But here initiation reaches its limit. Or, rather, its degrees and mediations are imposed. The bloody energy of the barbarian race took centuries to become the ferment of the republican people. And the historian will have to consecrate a whole lifetime to bringing it back to life. The woman of the people will need at least two generations to raise herself to the level of the book she inspires. The same blood that she communicates to the work of her lover and master still beats too strongly in her veins for her to be able to concentrate on a book. Later, the historian will point out the solution: it is the daughter, given a new education that begins in the cradle, who will fulfill the promise too impatiently attached to the mother. The well-born young countrywoman should marry a distinguished worker from the city. Only her daughter will be able to unite with a scholar in a marriage of the spirit.

Thus the initiatory circle cannot be closed for the historian and his mistress-servant. And the fact that Michelet comes *from* the people now assumes another sense. However "populist" his domestic behavior can be called, however much his public speeches and private acts of charity attest the link he has maintained with the people, the core of the problem becomes all the more evident. He who comes *from* the people is no longer *of* the people. He can only return to the people by the detour of the book. But what guarantee can the book have without the living return to the people who inspire it, without closing the circle of initiation?

The commentator, to tell the truth, does not exactly invite us to take the problem seriously. After all, he recalls, reverting to the tone of impertinence, these theories of a lover-pedagogue are also retrospective justifications of all-too-human behavior. "In throwing himself into these love affairs on the side, Michelet celebrates them as the Greek poets did Zeus's assiduities in pursuit of mortal women."[8]

You can hear the pedagogue speaking, trying to control the verbal inflation that is what pedagogy itself feeds on, to recall at the proper moment that words, after all, are only words, and that we shouldn't give them too much credence. But perhaps we should instead see these stories of love between two worlds as something other than classical reminiscences providing euphemisms for the weakness of the flesh and the academician's love affairs. Perhaps, in fact, they touch a much deeper point, which we might call the erotics of historical discourse. In any case, there are a few significant passages in Michelet's work that do speak of Greek poets and the earthly loves of Zeus. One example can be found in the lines of the *Origines du droit français* that begin what is intended to be the juridical biography of man. In the beginning is the newborn child, the exposed child abandoned to nature by his father:

Human scrap, cast off into nature, he was often welcomed by her. This rude mother adopted him, strewed leaves over his cold bed, rocked him with the north wind, fed him with wolves' milk and lion marrow.

And yet what were the mother's laments? They alone could say. The very stones cried for them. Ocean himself was moved on hearing Simonides' Danaë.[9]

As we know, Danaë's lamentations are those of a mortal punished for surrendering to Zeus's seductions. Her father locked her and the infant Perseus, son of the golden shower, in a wooden ark and cast it into the sea. But Perseus is not only the scandalous fruit of a guilty love. If his grandfather exposed him to the justice of the waves, it is because the oracle foretold, just as it did to Laius, that the infant would one day kill him. Perseus is the brother of Oedipus and Moses, children exposed and marked by the fate of parricide. Here the story of the origins of law is, properly speaking, the originary story of the subject's relation to the law and to discourse. But Perseus will have the calmest of such destinies: he will not marry his mother, and he will kill his father only in an accident that has no consequences. The myth of Perseus offers a minimal version of the wound that founds the speaking subject, and this is indeed what Michelet's account emphasizes: Perseus goes off with his mother to be nestled within a nature that has compassion for a mother's suffering and welcomes abandoned children. Nature speaks for the mute mother; nature's tears and emotions accompany the mother who accompanies her child. There is no abandoned child who is not received into nature's maternity, no suffering unredeemed or speech deprived of meaning. The adventure of Danaë and her child gives history its mythology, the *logos* of its story. It gives this *logos* a foundation in this first story of the stone and the ocean that speak, in the primary expressiveness of nature, an expressiveness that is exactly identical to its capacity to receive and welcome, following the first homonymy of the Greek *legein*.

The historian's discourse is thus founded upon a maternal theory of meaning: a theory of the symbolism of mother nature, who gives shelter to the abandoned child and gives voice to the unspeakable lamentations of the woman. The historian is a son who returns to the maternal source of meaning, who becomes a child once again to recover "the deep inner point at which instinct unites all life." In this autumn of 1842, the union with Marie-Barbara confirms for him what he was already beginning to sense: the great primary, feminine symbolism of speaking nature, of meaning attached to its primary expressiveness as a child is to its mother. Forgetful man must return to this source for his virile work of analysis to be like a sculptor's chisel, revealing the living form, rather than like a scalpel that only confirms death.

What is at stake, then, is not the weakness of the flesh and the literary references that provide euphemisms for it, but rather the stories historians tell and the order of meaning that provides their foundations. Love affairs on the side and their "celebration" take on a role within the movement of returning to the source; it is a resource for the historian who must decipher the living tradition written on the mute body of the people: the passage from primary maternal rusticity to civilization, progress, and democracy. But this resource turns out to contain a paradox: it is possible to return to Saint Genêt or Saint Éloi, to suppress the distance that separates us from what no longer exists, thanks to this resource of the people, of the simplicity found at home. But the distance from contemporaneous simplicity, there under one's own roof, remains insurmountable. The lover cannot finish the historian's labor, initiate her who initiated him. There is no individual solution to the problem of the education of simple folk—of the people and of women. The problem is general and concerns the gap, the absence of a common language between the educated classes and the popular classes. The only resolution will be a social one, and whatever the historian has to contribute to it will come not only from his books but also from his work as a teacher. But he cannot teach his own servant; he can only teach her teacher, the mediator who must reestablish the link between classes. This mediator is the young man, the son who is no longer an infant—a being without language—and not yet a bourgeois or a worker enclosed in the language of his specialty, in the narrow constraints of the division of labor.

Having been welcomed and received by his mother and by nature's maternity, the time has come for him to pay his debt to the mother, to woman in general, to the power of love, of nature and the true people. Thus in the winter of 1847–48, the professor speaks to his students of the drama of separation and confides in them the mission of reconciliation, and the weapon to accomplish it. This weapon is love. The language that is needed to bind the classes together is the language of the bond in general. What is missing between the poor and the educated is what makes for a bond in general, among the rich as among the poor: love.

This is why the mission of the young student from a good family is no different from the mission of a young man in general. The introduction of Michelet's *L'Amour* is addressed to a young man, a worker or student. In the age of the division of labor, the notary and the scholar are workers just like the locksmith or the carpenter; they are men of a specialization, smiths whose backs are bent from striking their own particular iron. To breathe and take heart, they need to drink once again from the eternal waters of woman/nature, at the cost for each of raising up the woman who raises him up, of leading her "into his own world, his path of new ideas and progress, the path of the future."[10]

Even he whose social condition has no importance can be given a proper name. Quite naturally, the professor of love will give him the name of the young man in general, the name of Danaë's son, Perseus. To deliver his mother, Perseus must deliver the woman in general: Andromeda, the woman-child, the petrified woman, chained to her rock. Andromeda is the power of nature that is still a prisoner of nature, a prisoner of the cycle of blood that makes her permanently sick, a prisoner of the forces of incarnation that hold her within the primary symbolism of nature. The sick woman must be protected; the captive woman must be liberated in order to express her power to renew life in the element of justice and freedom. The young man, Perseus, must accomplish the separation, cut the bond that petrifies woman, that encloses her in the immediacy of nature. But the young man must also welcome her whom he detaches from the rock into the double maternity of the couple.

For this is, in fact, the primary signification of maternity: the act of welcoming. In preaching love and maternity, Michelet is not, as Zola would do later, calling for a joyous proliferation to fecundate the national future. The woman's maternity fundamentally works on her husband. It is first of all the power of the home and of the arms that welcome the worker worn out and atrophied by his labor, it is the Lethe, the source of love and renewal whence he must drink every day to recover his power of creation and love. The child is no more than the perpetuation of the relation that is forever accomplished in the time of its own present. Marriage is an end unto itself. Every day, the man gives new birth to the woman by his labor, and the woman gives new birth to the man by her love. Each exercises, for the other, the daily function of giving birth to a human being living in love and freedom. And this would even seem to be a privilege granted only to poor couples. The rich couple is always exposed to malicious, predatory third parties who come between the woman and the husband-child: confessor, confidante, or servant. There should be no servants in the home. The professor of love who dismissed Barbara to placate his daughter, then Rustica to placate his second wife, excludes servants in general from the house of the young Perseus. The servant was only an expedient for the scholar and widower who had wandered too far from the source of the woman and the people. But at the source there are no servants, only women and children. And there is no education possible outside of the maternal-conjugal relation, for only love educates. Make haste, young Perseus!

But here we catch a glimpse of how deeply rooted the evil is. The professor calls upon love to fill the gap between rich and poor, between the people and the scholars. But it turns out that the evil exists not only between classes, but also in the very place where one had hoped to find the remedy, the principle of the bond. Rich or poor, student or worker, the young man no longer wants to love, he no longer wants to liberate Andromeda. A never-before-heard rumor starts to circulate: "We do not want to love! We do not want to be happy!... There's something suspicious under there."[11] Such is the new way of thinking: there is an underside of things we must be wary of. And thus does young Perseus act. He mistrusts love and seeks only pleasure. He ignores the prisoner's appeal and follows instead the call of the sterile masculine band that knocks on his door: "We're all waiting for you. We're off to the Chartreuse, to the Chaumière, to the Lilas.... Amanda, Héloïse, and Jeanneton are coming too."[12] The final bill for this pleasure is paid off by abandoning the woman: not merely the unhappy fate of a girl seduced and abandoned but the separate existence of the two sexes as a new and fatal form of social life.

This is the previously unheard-of evil that the moralist, at the beginning of *La Femme*, shows to an audience of young bachelors—to men, that is, grown old before their time. He analyzes the condition of the abandoned woman on the basis of the dissection of one of these victims. In the course of the winter of 1858–59, the historian, tired of "listening to prattle," decided to actually push his project to its conclusion: make the mute speak, know the outside by the inside, life by death. Young Doctor Büchner despaired of the infinite dissection necessary for one being to ever be able to know another. As usual, to base reasoning on one's own knowledge makes things more difficult. Whether more lucky or more practical, the historian of the people was able to read the cadavers dissected by Doctor Béraud like open books. In the richly decorated volutes of the brain, he read, he *heard* the language of truth that is usually hidden behind the coarse surface of the human face. And thus he came to be a witness to one of those singular facts of anatomy that are capable of opening an infinite world of reflection for the moralist.

> This infinitely rare singularity was a fairly large calculus found in the womb. This organ is often somewhat dried up these days but never to this point, which indicated a quite extraordinary state. In the sanctuary of life, abundance, and fertility, that there should be this cruel desiccation, this desperate atrophy, this Arabia, if I dare say, this rock... , that this unfortunate woman should have been turned to stone... threw me into a sea of somber thoughts.[13]

The body of the petrified woman ended up on Doctor Béraud's table in March, a month of springtime and fertility that unhappily is preceded by carnival and its sterile debauchery. And our first thought might be that this is the body of some Amanda or Jeanneton abandoned by her young man after a night of pleasures at the Lilas or the Chaumière. But the finely decorated volutes of the brain were enough to set aside that hypothesis. It wasn't carnival that led the unhappy girl to the hospital and then the morgue. Doubtless the misfortune of a seduction in some provincial town overpopulated with bachelors forced her to come to Paris to hide her shame and her child. But the suffering of abandonment is more than the suffering of betrayal and infamy, since it deprives us of a person and a place to welcome us. Having found work in Paris as a laundress, the only place she could find to sleep was a closet under her employer's stairs. And it was there that, on account of coal smoke, she caught the light fever that, had she only a home, would have cured by a few days in bed. But without a home you are condemned to the hospital and it was there that she died. She died not of vice, disgrace, or despair, but simply of the abandonment that turned her into a woman without a man. Her inglorious fate, to that extent, is exactly the same as the apparently more honorable fate of the young woman who, to prepare for her exams and make her own way in the world, devoured the "thick and compact little books where all science is concentrated in a dry, indigestible form, like a rock."[14] The evil lies in the egotistical reign of *calculus* which condemns the woman to solitude. Like Littré, Michelet recognizes only a single word where our dictionaries distinguish between the art of counting and the stony concretion that dries up organic life. The age of calculus is an age of petrification. The desertification of the uterus is the drying up of the dual relation, the double maternity where

THE POOR WOMAN 83

one gives birth to him or her who gave birth to you.

To struggle against this abandonment is not simply the demand of a moralist. The eloquent death of the laundress and the mute life of the student bear the same testimony: where the woman is alone, the book is a stone. The historian's book and the sexual organs of the poor woman are condemned to be petrified together if the source dries up. The historian, too, has the task of giving birth to her who gave birth to him. He crosses back over the river of the dead, makes the voices speak from the grave, gives new life to the mother who gave him his life. And he does so in order that his listeners or readers will in turn take care of their common mother. Thus his work as an individual is inscribed within the work of time. It participates in the movement of rebirth that should nourish the virile France of the democratic age with its rustic and barbarian maternity. But this movement of making death fertile is struck with the century's contradiction. On the one hand, the historian uncovers the positive signs of this rebirth of death by evoking the way that the taste for flowers and the cult of the dead have developed together since his childhood. In the middle of the corruption of this bachelor century, he has seen the signs of a new hope: hortensias and dahlias in flower beds, flowers and visitors in cemeteries.

> I can recall very clearly that a cemetery at that time was an Arabian desert where no one went. Today it is a garden full of monuments and flowers. The increase in wealth certainly plays a role but so does the progress of the heart. For people do go there; the poor find a way to bring wreaths and keepsakes. At the important moments of the

year, the wife of the poorest laborer finds a few economies in the household groceries in order to bring some flowers to the dead.

Death is the sister of Love. These two religions are related, indestructible, eternal. And if Death lives, why not Love as well?[15]

The sisterhood of death and love thus weaves together the links between the historian's work and the poor couple. The laborer's wife economizes the few cents that allow the ancestors' tomb to flourish. She also knows how to bring a few flowers, live or printed, into the home in order to make it desirable for her man, to make him want to stay there and install himself in the reciprocity of the maternal relation. The historian, however, draws the flowers of life out of stone. He unchains Andromeda from her rock, liberates the maternity of meaning, the better to be able to draw the voice of ancestors from the grave and vegetation from the tree of life, the better to ensure the transition from barbarian France to the democratic nation. But this work of living death, this enterprise of the story that welcomes in order to gather, depends on the social consistency of the sexual relation that is a relation of double maternity. The reversibility of death is supported by the reciprocity of love. The living death of the cemetery in flowers and of the book fertilized by the return to the source attest that love still can live. But love must complete the proof and in turn make it possible for the cult of the dead and the historian's work to continue. The consistency of the amorous bond and the couple's daily crossing of Lethe are all that ensures this life of love, without which the life of death perishes. To bring forth new flowers on graves, the historian must constantly return to an always living source. But this is the heart of the contradiction. The same century that puts flowers in cemeteries and transforms their Arabia into a garden condemns the flower of life, the womb of the woman of the people, of the woman-people, to the solitude of the desert, the stoniness of Arabia. The great sickness, the great scourge of the age, succeeding upon the leprosy and plagues of bygone days, has been identified. The century suffers from illnesses of the womb—illnesses of abandonment and petrification, of the calculating and calcifying egotism of bachelors that has made inroads even among the poor.

Giving the servant her leave only makes the century's contradiction more apparent and thus makes more imperative the task of reconciling the logic of the work with that of the amorous and domestic order. The fate of history as a complete figure, as a discourse that leaves no stone sterile, no grave mute, no sentence without meaning, depends on the incessant reciprocity between the order of discourse and the order of the family. At the moment when social knowledge is being constituted as a new discursive figure, Michelet's crusade bears witness to the fact that there is no novelty in knowledge that is not sustained by some kind of eroticism. The historian's science is, first of all, an art of love.

Marthe and René

Perhaps we should change the scene if we want to understand this better. The next letter is a real one. The poet who wrote it has no woman of the people at home. He is a foreigner without many resources. To tell the truth, he has no home. For the moment he is living in a hotel. He met the poor woman on the street; she was sitting on the ground, her head in her hands, at the corner of the rue Notre-Dame-des-Champs. He walked more quietly when he saw her. "When poor people are thinking," he tells us, "they shouldn't be disturbed."[16] But there may be another reason: the fear of what he will see when the frightened woman lifts her head and her face stays stuck on her hands.

Thus does Rainer Maria Rilke present the discretions and fears of Malte Laurids Brigge. But at least once he himself stopped at such a sight. This is how he met Marthe, a seventeen-year-old working girl, and helped her out of extreme poverty. After he'd made some connections, he found a protector for her. And at Duino, as a guest of Princess Marie von Thurn und Taxis, he received from

THE POOR WOMAN 87

Marthe a piece of paper with just a few lines written on it, the most beautiful love letter—it is the princess herself who tells us so—ever written to a poet. Still, when he goes back to Paris, the night of love that he recounts to the princess is a strange one.

> You ask about Marthe; I have only seen her twice, though the first time the whole night long. It was *mi-carême*, two days after my arrival; I traveled out to Sceaux, Frau Woermann was away, so I went into the park and knocked at the Russian's studio.... Marthe rushed out, bending forward like a fleeing doe, a gold band round her temples, wearing a kind of Greek garment—engulfed by the size of her own eyes.—It turned out that she wanted to go to Paris and dance; she had done nothing all day long but wash and arrange her hair and dress up and all the time, so she said, she felt that she was not doing all this only for the ball, but for something much more important. The night was sad, I took her to Bullier, we missed the last train to Sceaux, my flat was not yet furnished, so we drifted about on the streets until morning and in uninviting cabarets, in horrid surroundings (it was my fault for not knowing any better places!). She had insisted on going with bare feet and sandals, so as to be properly Greek: that made her appear improbable and pathetic (something like a beggar-maid in Heaven). At Bullier's and on the street, where she walked, wrapped and draped in her tunic, with strangely tiny steps, picking her way through the confetti that covered the ground and drifted about like many-colored snow, people looked at her in surprise,

shyly, I might even say with a kind of timid respect. She was so entirely different from all those others and their dogged, facile amusements. Among all those more or less sordid women she appeared like a dying child who would be a Saint a few years after her death.[17]

There are several ways to read this story. One would be to adopt Michelet's point of view. Right away we could recognize the classic scene of perversion in which the young man and the girl of the people both lose their way. The young man—a foreigner who lives in Paris like a provincial student—has led the little seamstress who hangs out with bohemians, lives with a Russian painter, and goes out with an Austrian poet to the Bullier dance hall, which used to be called, and will be again, the Closerie des Lilas. The scene takes place during carnival, and the rest of the story is well known.

Still, the poor woman here takes on a somewhat disconcerting aspect and enters into a singular relationship with the young man. Instead of Amanda, Héloïse, and Jeanneton, who accompany the band of bachelors to the Closerie, there is this Marthe, named after a holy woman and resembling a Greek statue or a figure in a stained-glass window—a dying child, almost a saint.... In the middle of the sentence, the poet shifts from German to French to emphasize the "kind of timid respect" that makes Marthe a foreigner amid the Jeannetons and Amandas whose amusements are so dogged and facile. And how could we compare the behavior of students out on a spree with the singular attitude of the poet, this relationship that hangs upon the desire of another that does not know itself? "It turned out that she wanted to go to Paris and dance ... and all the time, so she said, she felt that she was not doing all this only for the ball, but for something much more important."

At this, of course, the friend of the people would share the mocking laugh of the man of the world about that "much more" and the quasi-vaudeville that sends this couple wandering through streets and cabarets because they lack a place to consummate the ordinary consequences of going to Bullier's during carnival. Even swearing to the fundamental chastity of this desire for much more would not save the couple from opprobrium. For in this excess of desire over the simple weakness of the flesh, Proudhon (Michelet's brother on questions of the people and women) identified the principle of feminine idealism, a much more frightening thing than the brutality of male egotism. However chaste the relation between the poet and the working girl might remain, it represents a far worse perdition than simply being abandoned to a seducer: the vertigo of someone leaning over a lake to seek their own image. The lake is not the mirror of the *grisette* doing her makeup for the ball; it is the obscure place where that desire that cannot know itself is born. Sterile death is the end of this movement of a body that withdraws in the purity of looking at and listening to the place and the name of its desire: "engulfed by the size of her own eyes ... *she wanted to leave this world in order to be completely absorbed by my eyes and my ears; she bent over me like a little girl seeking her own reflection in the lake, even at the risk of drown-*

ing there."[18] In this mortal desire to decipher her own image—her enigma—in the gaze and speech of the other, a Michelet (but also a Hugo, a Proudhon, or a Zola) would recognize the perversion that menaces the woman or the worker who goes astray: the taste for a singular enjoyment to be found in the gaze and speech of the other, just like the enjoyment that Désirée Veret, Reine Guindorff, and their fellow seamstresses once found in sermons of the Saint-Simonians—at the risk of meeting death at the end of one's desire—the desire of the other—of drowning, like Reine the seamstress, no longer in the other's gaze but in the cold waters of the Seine.[19]

Eighty years later, Marthe is indeed their sister; like them she is torn between the world of work and the world of speech. And the poet, of course, at the cost of one or two odd turns of phrase in French, says it better than we can:

She cannot foresee any kind of life for herself, at the moment she seems to perch on the back of that other life like the little heron in Egypt who lives on the back of cows. Having worked since she was four years old, doing all the little jobs that fall through the boards of the professions, she cannot see any work that she could do and every path seems barred by the heavy shadow of the "boss" which has to be traversed with one's eyes closed if one wants to find profitable and enduring employment.[20]

The working girl who doesn't work is certainly the proper companion for a poet who doesn't write, who is desperately waiting for the return of the voice that comes

THE POOR WOMAN 91

from the obscure site of creation and that will allow him to continue the *Elegies* that he started that winter at Duino. In the relation between these two idlers, in the double suspension of their desire, the gaze of the friend of the people would recognize the evil that goes far beyond any student wildness and which is nothing more or less than the complete dissolution of any bond. The delay in the delivery of furniture that leaves the consequences of the ball unresolved is no simple accident: it is precisely the absence of any relation of welcoming between the young man and the poor woman. The poet has no place for the working girl who is herself homeless: she lives—like a sister, of course— with the Russian or rather Siberian painter in a studio/ dormitory that is "*in such a state of untidiness that one would call it a landscape if it happened to in the open air. They sleep on pallets among a heap of things that have been strewn around or forgotten.—Marthe very proudly showed me the hyacinth bulbs that began to sprout under the blankets in the innocent warmth of her poor little feet.*"[21]

There is no need to know that Hyacinth, Apollo's too jealous lover, is the son, the lost child, of Clio, the muse of history, to recognize in Marthe's studio the strict caricature of the home that the working woman should make flourish in order to keep the thirsty smith at home. The relation of double maternity finds its parody in this ambiguous sorority that terminates in a parodic maternity, a doubtful virgin fertilization. The young working girl who lives on the back of another life offers the poet the pure figure of nonrelation, of the impossibility of reciprocity and the discourse that it sustains. This impossibility is no longer merely the deferred initiation of the woman of the people by the learned man. Apparently, the poet has no problem of literacy to resolve. Despite having begun to work at the age of four, Marthe seems to have found the time to learn to read and write. And while the poet is recounting their night together to the princess, he has lent the young girl a book to help her bide the time, a thoroughly edifying piece of high literature: *L'Annonce faite à Marie*. The impossibility of a relation between the poet and the poor woman is not one of initiation into culture.

But neither does the impossibility of the relation consist in the simple distribution that Rilke had set forth in an earlier work, *The Book of Poverty and Death*, where one finds a clear opposition between true and false poverty. On one side the sterile poverty that is simply lack of wealth, the poverty all too evident in the dereliction of cities: the men sneaking around the hospitals, worn out from their spiritless service of meaningless things; the children who do not hear the call of flowers; the young women who close up; the dingy maternity wards that are an anticipation of death, of a bad death, a death hanging green and bitter like a fruit that will never ripen. On the other side there is an essential poverty, incarnated in the *poverello* of Assisi, the poorhouse that is an altar in which "the eternal transforms into food," a child's hand seizing the seashell, the cup, or the beetle, a bit of earth that is a fragment of a future crystal.[22] These poor, "like guards of draped-off treasures / they keep safe but never saw themselves,"[23] represent a continuation, passing through Symbolist asceticism, of the Romantic tradition of the *simple folk* who possess the essential forces of life and assure the rest of a world in which things and deeds are reduced to their essential nature. The tranquil fertility of this world can still be identified with a primary meaningfulness that does not suffer from any gap between the name and the thing, any wound to the speaking being:

> Then there remains not even one scar
> of their name upon their body, prepared to sprout
> and bedded like the seed of that seed
> from which you stem forevermore.[24]

This is the poverty that guarantees the advent of he whom the poet serves, he who will give birth to death—good death, the great death that every man bears within himself, the ripe fruit of which he is no more than the hull.

But the meeting with the Parisian working girl will muddy this image of muzhiks and icon-painters that was formed on the banks of the Volga. This Marthe who is neither a housewife nor a streetwalker, who only sits listening to the poet like Mary at the Lord's feet, symbolizes neither the desolation of industrial cities nor the essential fertility of simple folk. She bears within herself neither the sterile death of those whose life fritters away between the foundling hospital and the asylum, nor the personal death that takes root and grows in the furrows of mother nature. She is "futureless," a pure looking and listening, who, seeking to decipher herself in the poet's look and voice, refers him back to his own enigma, his own solitude—to that mountain of stone into which he must advance until he himself has no essence other than stone, constantly having to resist the desire for someone, some loving woman, to come and cut him out of the mountain and carry him away to a meadow full of cyclamens in bloom.[25] It is appropriate for the sculptor to be walled in. He who cannot be protected cannot be a protector either. He must renounce the role of the teacher in love. Before "that generous little creature who could have been a source of unbounded delight and help to someone whose nature is less cautious and not so endangered" as his, he can only "let things take their course and go take a look now and then."[26] The impossible consistency of the relation is not a question of intellectual and social distance; it lies in its very nature. The poet's relation to the poor woman is no different than his relation to any woman, than the relation of any man to any woman. The maladroitness of the man who cannot find an appropriate place for his night of love is also the absence of a place for a relation between two equally abandoned beings. Love as double maternity, as envelopment of one another, is impossible. Equally impossible is the pedagogy that allows the other to advance on the path of common knowledge and language. What is possible is to grant the other some space, some silence, the conditions that will allow his or her own fruit, his or her own death, to ripen. Each of us can only give birth to death on his own behalf. The life of death cannot be transmitted, taught, or told. The ripening of death is the solitary labor of each one of us.

The suspended relation between the poet and the working girl allows us to see that the discourse of the historian

THE POOR WOMAN   95

and friend of the people stems from a whole series of equivalences that may be lost but are always capable of being reawakened. The reversibility of life and death, the reciprocity of the couple, the communication between classes and generations depended on the common maternal nature of the sexual relation and the signifying relation. This common nature was expressed in the power of the narrative that welcomes and gathers, that is a science and an education. Opposed to this happy organization of meaning, the poetic act may be posed as the act of an impossible relation, the separation between the ability to speak truly and the satisfaction of a loving relation, between the art of writing and the art of love. The project of the teacher in love, of the historian of the people, is very precisely dismissed by two tercets in the nineteenth sonnet of the first part of *Sonnets to Orpheus*:

> Never has grief been possessed,
> never has love been learned,
> and what removes us in death
>
> is not revealed.
> Only the song through the land
> hallows and heals.[27]

The solitude of song undoes the knot that ties together the arts of loving and of learning. Writing to Benvenuta, the poet must reaffirm—and this is not merely an alibi to hold at bay this woman who threatens to overwhelm him with her love—that Eros is neither rich nor beautiful, and that he bears within himself no promise of reconciliation.[28] Of course, such an affirmation is not sufficient to dissipate the great myth of maternal nature, the anxiety of the child who would like to return into oneness, the fantasy of liberated sex recovering the innocence of childhood, the cataclysmic and catastrophic meetings with substitute mothers, lovers in whose hands the poet's hands seek refuge, resting like John on Elizabeth's heart or Jesus on Mary's.[29] Even if the poet returns to his essential solitude every time, the poem itself continues to refer to the myth of a harmonious totality in which each thing and each being would find its place, in which the word would attain the fullness and flavor of the fruit that speaks both life and death in the mouth. And the *Open* in which things thus reach their exact center of gravity is still defined as the community of the living and the dead. Only he who has raised his lyre among the shades, eaten the poppies of the dead, can gain the knowledge of the image, the ability to make the slightest sound resonate without becoming lost. He alone can express the sweet and eternal voices of the double realm.[30] But the statement of this condition is every bit as much the mark of its impossibility. Only the angel circulates between the two realms. But the angel cannot be identified with any power to bring beings together. On the contrary, he is the infinitely distant. The scene of the community thus remains the pure space of the poem. There is no social relation, no home that corresponds to it. A comparison between the angel of the poem and Michelet's vision of the witch shows how complete the reversal is: Michelet's witch remained a domestic genie, the misunderstood and slandered angel of the home. On the other side, Rilke's angel grants the exact touch of words only at the cost of solitude, of abandonment accepted. The poem is a mourning for the social relation, just as the proclamation of the social relation is a mourning for the poem.

This requires us to read the other side of Michelet's utopia tying the maternal discourse of history to the realization of the relation of love among the people. It is well known that Michelet shared with Proudhon a keen hatred for literary types and "literature." It would be hasty to think that this hatred can be simply reduced to the prosaic consciousness of the man of the people who commonly rejects empty words and unproductive beings. It is not a utilitarian principle that commands this hatred of literature. And it is not "popular sentiment" that refuses aesthetic enjoyment. For what is rejected is not aesthetic enjoyment but the enjoyment of words, more precisely their open and declared enjoyment. What the songful prose of the friend of the people indefatigably proposes is the identification of the end of the poem with the advent of poeticized life: the cult of the dead and that of the home, the woman of the people become the poetical angel of the abode, decorating the place of welcoming with flowers: dahlias or hortensias in flower beds, bouquets in vases, printed flowers on the wallpaper, tablecloths, and window curtains; printing become impression, the decoration and ambiance of a life all in flowers.... Michelet's domestic dream is echoed by Proudhon's social dream: the gestures of labor will no longer simply be given a rhythm by song but will become the moments of a great Apollonian festival, the cultivated earth will become an immense garden and labor a concert without end.[31] For Michelet and Proudhon the evil is not aesthetics, the glorification of the sensible. The evil is separation. When the people and love exist in their element, when existence becomes poetry, then the poem will become unnecessary: the poem, that is, the deceptive conjunction that threatens to tip over into nothingness at the end of each line and after the last verse.

Indeed, however ardently the poet may aspire to primary unity, the poem can only begin with separation. It is only a *eulogy*; it is not the *logos* that welcomes and gathers. The poet knows that he can only *hear* the wellspring where the dead drink and that what can be said by the singer can be heard only by the divinity.[32] He shows us the great fable, the great myth—the speech that says the thing, that *is* the welcomed thing—but he does so to manifest its radical strangeness. Pronouncing the great myth, he stops it at the edge of each line and at the final period of the poem. He surrounds it with the blank space of its impossibility. And this impossibility is nothing other than the irremediable division of voices and enjoyments that can never close their circle. Nowhere in the poem does the circle close, conclude; nowhere is the distance between the enjoyment of words and the possession of things and beings abolished. Prose, to the contrary, enjambs the line, chases away blankness, makes us forget myth by making it real. Prose gives a place, the most natural one of all, to the nonplace. This is why prose, in opposition to what the self-interested preachers of realism have always told us, is not the instrument of the pragmatic spirit or popular sentiment that repudiates the utopian mirage. For the modern utopia, in its very principle, is not the happy islands but the production of the *place* where separation is erased, where the order of discourse exactly and naturally corresponds to the order of things and their properties. Modern utopia works within realism and uses prose, which is a better liar than poetry. For who will ever bother to believe in the *Open*? But who will refuse to believe—if only for a minute, which is always enough—in the self-evidence of the hearth and the people, of science and labor, race and progress? Who will not believe all the more easily, since it is only a question of seeing and since the words flow continuously, bridging separation at each and every line, hiding the operation that pushes nothingness into visibility? What the poem dismisses, in fact, is the password that both poses and hides the image imposing *reality* as the place where words are adequate to *their* things. The poem turns toward the celestial constellation—the "Rider" of the eleventh sonnet of the first part of the *Sonnets to Orpheus*—only to tell us that even conjunctions of stars deceive us.[33] To this extent the poem—accused of fomenting all sorts of mirages—is what best denounces the modern utopia, this production of utopia that is not the dreaming of visionaries but the ordinary suture that holds together the discourse of politics or social science. If Michelet gives us a particularly exemplary version of this utopia, it is not in his grand enthusiastic expressions of national faith, but in the ordinary conjunction of words. Beneath his pen the historian's utopia becomes one with the end of literature. Literary excess is entirely absorbed into the ability to express a world in which there are only the living and the dead—none of those quasi beings produced by fiction—where all speech is the murmur of a well or the voice of a grave and makes manifest the configuration of a place or the state of a subject. One of Michelet's descendants will say that the historian "almost detests events." What he detests may not be so much the futility of battles as the event of the word that expresses no property. For him every fiction is a production, every conjunction of words or images a document, testimony to a certain state of affairs, of places and beings. Even if he never thinks about it, this belief inscribes the scholarly historian of our time within the utopia of a discourse without an exterior, of the narrative that gathers everything, that does not know the emptiness of words. Today's historian cannot do without the maternal fantasy of the social relation, any more than Michelet, the founding father who is always getting in the way, could do without the flowers on the hearth and in the cemetery.

The distant relation between the poet and the working girl, on the other hand, expresses both a general suffering of the relation—both social and amorous—and an ethical decision: to renounce loving, to renounce the energy that the writer of the previous century went to seek at the source, in the womb of the woman of the people, to know that conjunctions are only ever made of words and that the happy space of the word that strikes the perfect note comes only at the cost of accepting solitude.

Still, things are a little more complex. The time of this suspended relationship is also a time when the poet does not write, when he wanders from place to place in search of the lost thread of the *Elegies*. In this sense, the suspended relationship is also the nonplace of the poem itself. And to find the thread, the poet, like the historian, will have to dismiss the woman of the people: not in order to construct hearth and home but simply to enable the poem, in its very solitude, to come. For the poet who, with the break of 1914, lost Marthe at the same time as Paris, the autumn of 1919 presented a unique moment of suspense if not of choice. In Switzerland he had the opportunity to see Marthe again, and this occasion reawakened the old dream, the hope for hands that would close upon a reconciled life. A letter Rilke wrote while waiting for the meeting evokes the fullness, the overflowing of happiness that Marthe gave him, and adds:

> It will be almost a return to Paris for me, the meeting with this creature who knows about me with the deepest conviction; through her—even if it is only a few days I can spend with her—I shall soonest be able once more to heal the ruptured surface of my former life; Marthe's hands will hold the fractured end and the new beginning tenderly against each other.[34]

Once again, the poor woman's hands have been entrusted with reconciliation. But the three days Rilke spent with Marthe will give the lie to this hope. Of course, Marthe's heart has kept "all its geniality" and her artistic talents are in full flower. She is embroidering for the fall Salon a tapestry following a friend's pattern, which to the poet seems quite sketchy but which Marthe develops through the genius of her fingers that again and again find the correct thread without even looking. But Marthe has lost her voice, to the point where Rilke has difficulty understanding her. And her entire person is as if covered with a dingy veil, the mark of her family environment, "surroundings of such utter poverty that we cannot imagine, indeed can hardly describe them." Marthe herself was vainly tempted to describe it, before concluding: "*It's not even ugly—because there just isn't anything.*"[35] The royal poverty of the Greek statue has reverted to the unnameable poverty of those who are merely the not-rich. Marthe's hands were unable to hold together the end and a new beginning. "Her name has kept all its old resonances for me but it has not come back into my center even though her aspiration toward me was still just as absolute."[36]

Such is the account he sends to Lou Salomé, the first of the lover-mothers. And to Marie von Thurn und Taxis, the protectress of the *Elegies*, he addresses another conclusion in the form of a question: where should he live now? With the fissure not healed, Paris has become "impossible." And his review of possible places to stay sends us back to the fundamental quest: to find the "right place," the place of the *Elegies*. The poet does not say so, but we can understand it: the discovery of the right place for the poem passes through the dismissal of Marthe, through the awakening from the dream that gave him rest between the hands of the poor woman. Dismissing Marthe will always mean, at least symbolically, finding another fiancé for her. Symbolically, since as a matter of fact Marthe has found such a companion: the young artist whose tapestries she is making according to patterns that Rilke didn't appreciate but that others will—his name is Jean Lurçat. The symbolic dismissal is given in a strange letter—this one fictive—quite significantly finished in February 1922, just before the four feverish days that will produce the *Elegies*. *The Young Workman's Letter* will introduce Marthe as a fictional character within this fictive letter, which a young worker, initiated by a painter he met in Avignon, is supposedly writing to the poet V. (Verhaeren). The letter's tone is sounded by an accusation of a Nietzschean sort against Christianity and the religion of otherworldliness. Against the Christian culpabilization of sexuality, the young workman develops a utopia of liberated sexuality and recovered childhood. The genitals represent the one point where we have all remained children, the only remainder of the primary sexuality—the primary innocence—that was spread all through the child's body in agreement with mother nature.

At a turning point in this polemic, a little paragraph introduces a confession: "I am in love with a woman, hardly older than a child." There follows a description of this child-mistress in which we once again find Marthe, her provisional life—between the cracks of jobs, on the back of another life—her terror of the boss, and her interrogation in front of God, the "head boss." Thus Marthe, named as if in passing, is dismissed twice, becoming both a fictional character and someone else's companion—someone else from her own world, a worker. By delegation, as a matter of distancing along a chain, it is another poet, Verhaeren, the poet of the *Villes tentaculaires* but who also has been dead for several years, who becomes the confidant not of Marthe but of the supposed companion of a fictional Marthe. In the terms used at Bullier's, the terms that horrify the well-informed friends of the people even as they make them smile, we could say that he got rid of Marthe in the classic way, passing her along to another man. But there is both something more and something less here than this ordinary art of getting rid of one-time companions. On the one hand, the engagement with the young workman is only a fiction. On the other, the poet has also passed on to this imaginary laborer his fantasy, that of the reconciled body, of liberated sexuality, of the carnal recovery of childhood. This thought, which is his, and which has led him into the arms of both mother-lovers and girls of the people, must now be gotten rid of. It is time to say good-bye to the maternal sexual fantasy in order to be able to complete the work. This thought weighs the poet down, turns the energy of poetic separation away, toward the amorous lure of the reconciliation of the flesh. It weighs him down as the other's expectations weighed him down, as did the desire of the poor girl plunged in the poet's gaze and speech. The young workman, in taking on both Marthe and the sexual utopia, clears a place. Once Marthe has been dismissed, rendered imaginary, sociologized, the poem can come.

A Child Kills Himself

A wintry sky above the landscape of a working-class suburb. A woman seems out of place there. Her height accentuates the elegant cut of her coat and the distinction of her gait. She is coming out of an anonymous apartment block, one of those new but already dilapidated buildings where the city's poor now live. She is waiting for the tram, which takes a while to come. To pass the time, she looks the other way. For the landscape of this anonymous suburb is itself divided. There are the working-class apartment blocks and there are vacant lots along the riverside where wandering children play. The foreign woman stares intensely at a confused spectacle near the riverside. She does not know, we do not know, that at this very moment she is losing her way.

The film is called *Europe 51*. The actress who plays the foreigner is a foreigner herself. Her name is Ingrid Bergman. The director, a native who frames the foreigner's gaze on the suburbs of his city, is named Roberto Rossellini. They both know, no doubt, that in filming this scene of getting lost they themselves are losing their way, telling the story of their own perdition, that is, succeeding at the particular form of perdition that is known as creating a work [*œuvre*].

How should we understand this perdition? *Europe 51*, a film entitled with a place and a date, can easily be described as the representation of a trauma. First of all the trauma of an age and a civilization: the heroine, a rich bourgeoise absorbed by social life, was unable to see the true extent of the effects of this time of war and horror on her son, an impressionable child. The child's suicide tears her out of the complacency of her universe and sets her on a voyage into the heart of poverty and charity, creating a scandal that will lead her friends and family to have her committed. It is also a properly psychoanalytic trauma, as can be seen through a more precise analysis that shows how the story unfolds according to the rhythm of three identically recurring scenes.[1] Three times, leaning over a bed of suffering, Irene, the heroine, finds herself touching heads with someone she cannot save: her son, having survived his fall but succumbing to an overdose of morphine; a prostitute, whom Irene helps in her death throes; an inmate of the asylum, who has just attempted suicide: the return of a single trauma, of an irreducible real before which Irene is powerless.

But the art of the filmmaker here shows us something more than the troubles of the times and the repetition of the unspeakable. *Europe 51* is a film about events, encounters, and reminiscences, and perhaps also a film about the work [*œuvre*] and its absence.

A film about events: a film that is capable of teaching us something about what "something is happening" means. The problem of cinematographic art, as we approach its centenary, can be stated fairly simply: is it possible for something to happen that is not already on the poster? Most often it is enough to see, on the walls of subway stations as the train stops and starts again, the poster that exhibits the low-angle shots of the horror film or the teeming colors of a comedy to know that nothing will happen on the screen that goes beyond the significations that are already on the wall. But here something happens. The film places itself not under the sign of trauma but under the sign of the event, under the sign of the intolerable: *a child kills himself.* What makes this intolerable is not the repetition of an impotence, but rather the apprenticeship of the unique power that goes forth to meet the event. We can understand this even at the level of the plot: from one scene to the next, from one distress to the next, something new happens, the same trauma is not repeated. The heroine comforts the dying prostitute, whereas her child died alone, by surprise. And she saves her suicidal companion. But this gain in power is above all reflected in her face. The film is the story of a face that reflects, a look that observes and distinguishes, accompanied by a camera that follows the work of reflection. *Europe 51* works on representation, on the way subjects change their manner of being one with their representation. The power that this labor makes evident can be named in good old Platonic fashion: it is the power of reminiscence, of recalling a thinking subject to his or her destiny. This movement of reminiscence is accomplished through the conjunction of three acts, three imperatives set in action: to know what was said, to go see somewhere else, to remember yourself.

To know what was said: to know how the event consists in *saying*, in hearing what speaking means. For the event is first of all what relates to the nothing, the *niente* that runs throughout the film, said first by the child who has no particular complaint to make, repeated at the end by the mother when the psychiatrist shows her blots to be interpreted and she sees *nothing*. A scandalous response that provokes the return response: what do you mean, nothing? To see nothing in the image that allows the patient to be diagnosed is to admit to a radical madness. *Nothing* has neither place nor reason to exist. It is a pure vertigo, a call for the void. And it is indeed the void that is at stake here, just as in another Rossellini film that is also defined by a place and a number, another story about a child killing himself, *Germany Year Zero*. The patricidal child allowed himself to fall into the void, succumbing less to remorse than to vertigo.[2] And once again it is vertigo to which the innocent child succumbs, in the emptiness in the middle of the stairwell. The same vertigo, but also a different one: no longer that of the words which made a nation mad, but that of an unspeakable grief. And just like his guilty brother from Germany, he first rehearsed his scene as in a game. In front of the mirror of maternal vanities, in the emptiness that frames her image, he staged the death act that will throw him into the void with a curtain tie. The event relates to nothingness, to the radical lack of any cause or good cause that would reattach it to the rationality of the profits and losses of a collective trauma. And this is why it can provoke the movement of reminiscence. By slowing it down, Rossellini has here given the event a form that ties it in a singular manner to the labor of reminiscence. At first we think that the child who threw himself into the stairwell is dead, but this turns out to be false. The surgeon reassures us and at the same time the mother about the consequences of the accident. Still, soon afterward, when we hear the nurse talking about morphine at the child's bedside, we have a premonition of what is to come. But in the entire ensuing scene between mother and child, the camera seems to give the lie to this expectation of death that will later return by surprise. It is the *après-coup* of the event that sets off the labor of reminiscence, a labor that hangs on a single question: "What did he say?" Not: "Why did he kill himself?" The latter is the obscene question, the question posed by the politicians who know in advance why the child killed himself: because there is war, poverty, and the disturbances of the time and of consciences. It is the question posed by people who make knowledge out of what others do not know, and for whom, as a consequence, what happens or what happened is of no interest. Death is enough to set explanation going. There is never a lack of deaths or explanations.

Here something else is at stake. An event has occurred. The child has killed himself or rather fallen into the void. And it is not a matter of knowing why he killed himself, but rather what he said about his vertigo. What sets the heroine, Irene, on the path to her truth is the mystery of the words that the child must have said at the hospital, the words that would have signified his act to her. She goes to ask these words from the one who heard them, her cousin Andrea, the scandalous relative of the family, the communist journalist. She goes to him to know what was said. And of course that means nothing to him. He knows what speaking means. What interests him is what is behind words: behind speech, what explains it; behind the individual pain that seeks its meaning in a child's sentences, the great social pain. Andrea knows the reasons of this pain and he knows that it will not be cured by words.

He will thus propose another journey to her who wants to know what the child said. He will propose a cure to the suffering mother: to go see, to learn the great suffering of others.

A guided tour. She takes the tram with him to the suburban apartment block where he wants to show her another sick child whose cure depends upon no word, no psychological problem, but simply upon the absence of the money needed for treatment. At the end of the tramway, the people. This is Rossellini's stroke of genius, compared to the derisory overload of decors and signs, characters and atmospheric effects laboriously set out by so many of his fellow filmmakers to get us to recognize, in family celebrations, at bistros and popular dances, in tender or violent refrains, in postures and accents, the people in person. Here there is neither dancing, bistro, or local color or accent. This last absence can be attributed to an entirely practical reason: the film is dubbed. Just like the fishermen's wives in *Stromboli*, these Roman proletarians speak English. The heroes of *Rome Open City* had originally been filmed as if in a silent movie since there was no sound equipment. But the hazards and constraints of production meet up with a more essential hazard and constraint. The voyage to the land of the people, like the voyage to Italy, is not linguistic. In Rossellini's films the voice does not belong to what is represented, it does not specify a body. The voice is a call or a response. Except that the call is never heard and the gaze must make up for its lack and orient the body toward its place. The voice that counts is the one that accompanies and comments upon this movement. Rossellini can thus dispense with the flavoring of lower-class accents, along with all the other incidental effects, in order to grasp and seize upon the essential: the people are first of all a way of framing. There is a rectangular frame that the camera cuts out; inside this frame there are lots of people. And that is enough. We have here a necessary and sufficient structure of representation: the people are represented by a frame that encloses a lot of people—a fundamental structure that pays off in sensible qualities that become moral ones, in characteristics of unhappiness that can be exchanged for bursts of happiness: people are crowded together, but that way they can stay warm and maintain solidarity. And, to make the representation complete, there also has to be someone excluded, or, to put it in scholarly terms, there must be a contradiction within the people. And here, in the framing of the people's always-open door, a suspicious neighbor appears. Contradiction passes through the field of vision and guarantees it.

This is what a visit to the people is: someone leads you, you take the tram all the way to the end of the line and all of a sudden everything is in the frame: the people, which is a way for many to occupy a little space. For Irene this tour is a voyage to what Andrea knows how to represent, he who teaches what is behind words and on the hidden side of society, the go-between who organizes tours of the people. For her the vision is stupefying: she sees something she did not know about, whose existence she had not even imagined. Among those of us who have studied just as Andrea has, at least some, of course, can recognize things: that is what we could have seen by taking the subway or some other kind of public transportation to the end of the line: in an instant, the frame where there is everything. The people in person is there, we've seen them, and theory is right. A certain use of sensory certainty provisionally fulfills the desire to know.

A voyage to the "other side" of society, whose existence is recalled to us from the very first words of the film: if Irene has arrived home late it is because the strikes have made things so difficult. This relation between the two sides, the words that speak this relation, are Andrea's business. He sends the patient on a cure, offers her a trip—a profitable one—to the other side of society. And he has available what makes the cure an education: the intelligible knowledge of the connection between the two sides. *Mettere in relazione*, he says, is what matters. The art of the go-between is the art of connection. Irene went to him to find out what was said, but, as we know, this is not what he's worried about. He is there to unveil. His mastery defines a certain regime of what is represented: there is something to see, something hidden. A double gap converts representation into knowledge: behind the words are the facts that prove them wrong; behind the facts are other words that explain them. The answer to the question "What is happening?" is always already given. There is another place, one which we also know and which is to be found at the end of the tour, when we come back from the tram ride, called the editorial office. There is a corner of a desk in the office, always covered with papers, where a gentleman, whom the employees call *dottore*, writes down what you need to know to put things in relation. This tinkering at the desk corner has a name. It is called the labor of consciousness (*coscienza*, he tells Irene over and over). This labor founds a new connection, a new mode of being-together. "We will do it together," Andrea tells Irene. *Nous mènerons la lutte des classes*, "We will carry on the class struggle together," comment the French subtitles. But the struggle is precisely secondary. What Andrea proclaims is what precedes the struggle and gives it its meaning—the meaning of connection. What is essential resides in the relation between the people of apartment block number 3 and the corner of the desk in the editorial office, in the scene of cure and education that passes through the knowledge of the two sides and their connection.

It is with respect to this social scene—this medical and educational scene—that something is going to happen, a second event. Irene is going to go see somewhere else. She is going to leave the frame, leave what the *dottore*, the go-between, knows how to represent. She has gone back to apartment block 3 by herself to see the child who has been cured thanks to her subsidy. This tour has no guide, but it does have a program. Once this program is accomplished she is on her way back to the tram, since she now knows the route. And all of a sudden she turns around. She leaves the frame, although not in the technical, cinematographic sense. The problem is not one of shots and countershots. It is not a problem of camera work, which would still be part of the art of relation. What is at stake here is not the camera but cinema itself. What is at stake is the artist, what the artist as such can show us: not a play between what is in and out of the shot, between voice-on and voice-off, but a *hors-lieu*, something outside of any place, and the encounter of a character with this *hors-lieu*, which, in subjective terms, is called a conversion. A conversion is not in the first place the illumination of a soul, but the twisting of a body called by the unknown. The artist Rossellini shows us the sensible action of this conversion, the action of a gaze that turns around and pulls its body along with it toward the place where its truth is in question.

In material terms, Irene has turned around. Down there, by the river's edge, a confused scene is unfolding. A body is being pulled out of the water and children are recklessly rushing to see what's going on. Irene responds to the call of a child who risks falling back into the water, but she also responds to the call of the river: less the call of distance than of a movement away toward her own loss. The call of a *hors-lieu*, of what was not part of the tour, tipping over into the unrepresentable. All of a sudden space becomes disoriented. The barrack where Irene leads the reckless kids back to a mother, who is as burdened with children as she is unburdened with a husband, cannot be situated in the

A CHILD KILLS HIMSELF

space of the tour. She has lost the way that led from apartment block 3 back to the tram and the center of the city, back to the other side and the place where the two sides can be related to one another. We are no longer *at home* in society, in the sort of social home that allows a visitor who has left her own home and world at the other end of the line to know where she is, to find a place for herself in another's home.

This is how her madness begins: she takes a step to the side, losing her way. The moment arrives when the call of the void has an effect but no longer makes sense. The time to connect, explain, and heal has passed. Now something else is at stake: to repeat the event, go look somewhere else, see for oneself. This is how one falls into the unrepresentable, into a universe that is no longer the society sociologists and politicians talk about. For there are a finite number of possible statements, of credible ways of putting together a discourse or a set of images about society. And the moment arrives when the border is crossed and one enters into what makes there be sense, which for that very reason does not itself make sense, so that one must continue to walk under the sign of interruption, at the risk of losing the way. No doubt there are more and less painful ways of getting lost, and not all of them lead to the asylum where Irene will be locked up on account of her inability to explain her conduct, to connect it with a discourse about society. But at the very least they all lead one who has left behind the categories of what can be said about society, about the people, about the proletariat, or some other representable thing of this sort, to the point where what comes back to us from what we say is that no one can see where we're going.

Walking under the sign of interruption, of the event and the words that, having suspended the ordinary course of things, now oblige us to go forward without turning back. Such was already the constraint imposed by the daemonic sign that obliged Socrates to stop at certain moments and then restart forward—start questioning and defying—under the sign of this interruption. At the time of its release, Eric Rohmer hailed *Europe 51* as a modern version of the trial of Socrates. But this Socratic presence is not only in the negative aspect of a society that judges and condemns what it does not understand; it is first of all in the relation between the event and reminiscence, in the sign of interruption that sets us walking another way, an interminable walk in the course of which the subject exceeds everything that it intelligibly could be said to be one with.

The conversion thus arrives at the place where the act of "consciousness" ought to have occurred. Measuring this gap also means, for the author of these lines, measuring the gap between two visions of the film. I saw it for the first time a quarter of a century ago, at the time of the great revival or, rather, reinvention of Marxism that is associated with the name of Louis Althusser, who set forth its first tasks: to pay attention to the simple gestures that are so natural that we neglect to reflect upon them—seeing, hearing, reading, writing.[3] My ambition was to conceptualize cinematic realism within this framework: not a realism of social content, however, as the gods of the camera who were then honored at the Cinéma Mac-Mahon or in the columns of *Cahiers du cinéma* were far removed from those shores. The realism I was after would somehow have to bring together Marx's text with the images of Minnelli's comedies or Anthony Mann's westerns. "Realist" *mise-en-scène* unveiled a determinate world through the sole action of a material system of looks, gestures, and actions that lived, focused on, and dreamed that world; an unveiling without mediation, without any signification imposed from the outside, coming to capture the network of gestures in a register of ideological signifieds. Meaning should have been the physical evidence on the screen of the relations between a certain man and a certain world; it should be entirely produced and manifested by the relations between the characters and their universe.

This is the basis on which I had seen *Europe 51*, judging that it was "half a great realist film." Half of one, I wrote, because the film went awry at the midpoint, precisely when the heroine walked up the steps of a church, after which she would consecrate herself to caring for a tubercular prostitute, the "suspect neighbor" of apartment block 3. Up until that point, I added, the physical evidence of the character corresponded to the social evidence of her experience. A bourgeois woman, displaced from her own world, discovered an unknown territory in which she tried to situate herself through a common system of gestures, the gestures of a mother. Once she had climbed the stairs, she was no longer a character climbing stairs but a saint. The material movements of the body were thenceforth captured by an ideological signification that transformed them into an itinerary toward sainthood and madness, following the famous Pauline equivalence of the cross that is folly in the eyes of worldly wisdom.

Still, seeking to reconcile what I had to say with the resistance the film posed, I had found a solution that I had taken over from an old trick of Marxist aesthetics: as was well known at the time, Balzac, a legitimist reactionary, nonetheless showed us, against his intention and through the force of his art, a realist vision of the world that implicitly sapped his reactionary ideology and the ideological foundation of the monarchical order. In the same way, Rossellini the materialist filmmaker contradicted Rossellini the Catholic idealist, showing us something other than what the latter wanted to say. In spite of himself, he gave us every means to understand how his heroine went astray on the path to salvation: not having been able to understand what she saw, to achieve consciousness of the social relations in which she was caught, she fell back into what was sainthood for the Catholic ideologue but that the materialism of Rossellini's camera revealed to be—for us as for the world, even if in a different sense—madness.

But there was still something in the film that resisted allowing the same trick of "consciousness" that it let us see being applied to it in turn. And perhaps spending a few years at the end of subway lines or in the labyrinth of the archives of workers' movements was a way of prolonging its effect, of walking under the sign of interruption by holding the artifice of an answer suspended. Seeing the film again after a quarter century, it seemed that the gap that leads to madness or sainthood is not the effect of the stairway that leads from the street of walkers to the church of saints, where the priests on display are filmed without any more complacency than the popes of Eisenstein the dialectician. The conversion is the movement off to the side, the first deviation at the end of the purposeful visit. For she who had been invited to look behind things, the break comes from looking to the side instead. At this precise moment, by her own act, Irene bids farewell to this famous consciousness that she seemed to me to lack. Later still, while talking with Andrea, the man of authorized scandal, he will repeat to her, patting her shoulder protectively, *coscienza, coscienza!* Irene bids farewell to this consciousness in the Socratic manner; she *lets it go*.[4] She says good-bye to this consciousness that fabricates itself by tying together representations at the corner of a desk, that goes along at the same speed and with the same repetitive procedures as the assembly line she describes to Andrea. It is thus completely impossible to oppose the lucidity of consciousness to the wanderings of a beautiful soul. If sainthood is shown to be a folly, it is in exactly the same way that consciousness is shown to be the homologue of the assembly line, the constrained and repetitive writing of the *dottore* when he comes back from his visits to the people.

The genesis of sainthood is thus not any revelation in the smoke of incense between the church's pillars, but the chance of the deviation that afterward leads little by little toward someone we must call our neighbor. Little by little, we have gone where we should not go, where we no longer know where we are. It is in this way that we become foreign to the system of places, that we become the action of our own reflection. Becoming foreign, this "Christian" way of proceeding is still analogous to Socrates' way, to the *atopia* that Socrates calls on when Phaedrus, the naive skeptic, asks him if he believes in the fabulous story that tradition ascribes to the place they are walking to. "If I disbelieved it," responds Socrates—or rather, if I was an unbeliever like our men of science—I would not be an *atopos*, someone who is dis-placed, an extravagant. Socrates' response links displacement with belief or, rather, trust (*pistis*).[5] It is likewise an act of trust that leads Irene out of the frame, displaces her. And her entire itinerary can be placed under these two categories of displacement and trust. It is not that the wind blows where it wills, the point of view of an Augustinian God and the director Bresson. Rather it is that the walker is always right to walk, that one is always right to go out, go see something to the side, continue to walk wherever one's own steps—and not those of others—lead. All teleologies and all imageries of coming-to-consciousness are founded on the certainty of a distribution: some people's mission is to speak for others who know not what they do. Such is the philosophy of the desk corner in the editorial office, the point of view of the go-between. A point of view of mistrust: behind things is where their reasons lie. And we know, moreover, what happens to go-betweens in the end: they change the object of their mistrust. They come to think that the people are not what they are said to be, that we have been deceived about them. And the reason for this deception lies in some unsavory stories behind the scenes, in the back rooms of the workers' party. The go-betweens denounce them and right-thinking opinion calls it intellectual courage.

A CHILD KILLS HIMSELF

In the face of such "courage," from which all acquiescences are made, the strangeness of faith is first of all that of trust. Trust affirms that no one can see for those who do not see and turn others' ignorance into knowledge. The problem is not that of knowing what one does. Whatever clever people might think, that sort of knowledge is usually pretty widespread. The problem is to think about what one does, to remember oneself. To the young delinquent whom she allows to flee, Irene says only: *think* about what you are doing! And he will indeed think about it. Here the morality of the story and the morality of the camera are equivalent: converting one's gaze means, in the strict sense, practicing a new kind of thoughtfulness or respect. The Christianity of Rossellini the agnostic—and the artist, as such, is an agnostic: he does not express faith; what he does is to establish a point of view—this Christianity turns out to be an equality of respect. This aesthetic and ethical practice of equality, this practice of egalitarian foreignness puts into peril everything that is inscribed in the repertories of society and politics, everything that represents society, which can only be represented under the sign of inequality, under the minimal presupposition that there are people who don't know what they do and whose ignorance imposes on others the task of unveiling. But the question is not one of unveiling but of encircling. Irene's gaze encircles. The halo of sainthood begins as the modesty of this labor of attention. A labor that singularizes self and other. The gaze undoes the confusion of what is represented—at the cost, of course, of another confusion, that of social identities whose distinction depended precisely upon the first confusion. The artist's labor is to focus on the labor of this gaze, to construct the point of view of foreignness: the conversion of a body and the voice that accompanies it. This construction, as we have said, cannot have anything to do with the typicality of the characters or with the production of the linguistic signs of difference. The constraints of dubbing only confirm a well-defined use of the voice. All naturalness and all local accents are banished so that the voice is reduced to its essence: the commentary that everyone can give about what he sees. This commentary does not have an accent, whether English or Italian, bourgeois or lower class, masculine or feminine. This does not mean that it is an indifferently translatable Esperanto, but rather that it is the bearer of the point of view of the foreigner that undoes national, social, and sexual types. The character of Irene simultaneously feminizes the visitor of the poor, Francis of Assisi, and the merchant (whose story gave Rossellini the "idea" for the film) committed to the asylum on account of having denounced himself for blackmarketeering. And Ingrid Bergman, the Swedish actress from Hollywood whose voice resonates, in an English immediately translated into Italian, with the words of the converted French Jew Simone Weil—but who is also the sinner who has brought the scandal of adultery into Catholic and familial Italy—carries this gaze of the foreigner to its most extreme radicalness.

It is in the perspective of such a way of looking that the day at the factory, in which Rossellini condenses the experience of Simone Weil's factory year, is conceived and represented. The heroine does not go to the factory in order to go to the people, to know their condition. She only goes there in someone else's place, to do a favor for the mother of the errant children, who wants neither to miss out on the chance for a day of love because of working nor to lose her job because of being absent. She goes there as a foreigner in another's place. In the eyes of those who, never leaving their own home, accuse passing visitors of not knowing how to measure what is meaningful and what is painful for the natives, this is not a good way to know anything. Rossellini, like Simone Weil, has the opposite point of view: the only "natives" are those who have become resigned, who have stopped looking. It is the foreigner's gaze that puts us in touch with the truth of a world. The factory that Irene visits is the site of an assault much like the one perceived a century before by a cabinet maker playing the foreigner in a railroad shop. "The noise of the foundry, the bitter smell of the coke, the oil spread over all the gears assault the observer's senses," he wrote.[6] What the foreigner perceives, in the noise and dirt of the factory, as the intolerable itself, is the assault upon the gaze. The factory is in the first place an uninterrupted movement that hurts the eyes, that gives you a headache. It is a constant and unceasing procession of sensory shocks, in which, along with the ability to look, the possibility of thoughtfulness and respect is lost. Irene will again find this same system in the electroshocks of the asylum. In any case, the asylum works just like society. In more or less gentle or violent forms, there are two fundamental techniques of society described by the film: shock and interpretation. On the one hand, the movement of the assembly line and the bursts of electricity; on the other, the Rorschach blots—the nothing that you have to say something about—to be interpreted, and the system of explanatory attributions and inferences that make up the audible discourses of the social, that create society. The factory, the newspaper, and the asylum weave together this rationality. The judge and the priest order us to acquiesce in it.

What is at stake in the struggle going on under our eyes is precisely the effort to liberate the gaze from the assault that both shock and interpretation lay to it, to restore to it the sovereignty that allows it to act, to determine the proper gesture. What sort of gesture should be made is the object of a nocturnal discussion between Irene and Andrea on the piazza of the Campidoglio. Irene has come to ask what the child said. Andrea turns back on her the stereotypes of explanation: the war, the world in ruins, and the disturbance of consciences. But Irene already knows that she must interrupt him and give another response: there is something else to be done, a gesture that she has not accomplished. Now, this question of the gesture is placed under the most august patronage possible: the equestrian statue of Marcus Aurelius, the *imperator* above all others, the stoic emperor, master of himself and the world. In front of this same statue, a hundred years earlier, another foreigner had stopped to meditate upon the virtue of the proper gesture, of the imperial sign: "In the center of the square stands a bronze equestrian statue of Marcus Aurelius. The attitude is perfectly easy and natural; he is making a sign with his right hand, a simple action that leaves him calm while it gives life to the entire person. He is going to address his soldiery, and certainly because he

A CHILD KILLS HIMSELF 127

has something important to say to them."[7] This little gesture, this simple action that leaves the actor calm, is for Taine the mark of the antique simplicity of both generals and sculptors, as opposed to the modern universe where princes are on display and artists have all agreed to reproduce the commonly *distinguished* air of horses and horsemen. A world of distinction and representation, of warm coats and rain boots, of nervous, feminine sensibility and dilettantes who avoid popular vulgarity for lack of knowing the gesture that makes the people peaceful and attentive.

Rossellini's film could be described thus: the history of a gesture, the gesture that brings peace and salvation, the gesture that failed at the beginning but will succeed at the end. How can we accomplish this little action that leaves calm and brings peace: a peace which is, of course, quite opposed to the techniques of pacification that stem from shock and interpretation. There is a gesture to be found, a right way of setting one's head against the head of someone else who is suffering. For it is precisely not the same thing, the same trauma, each time. The gesture is adjusted and gains in power, culminating in a final, scandalous, and atopian gesture. In the final shot, the madwoman enclosed behind the bars where neurotic women are treated makes a sign from above, like the *imperator*, but behind the bars of her window, to the people from the working-class suburb who have come to see her. Quite simply, she gives them her benediction. The correct gesture is the end of the journey, the memory of a wandering astray that has become an act of peace. In the asylum, as elsewhere, there is the possibility of peace in the face of the techniques of pacification, the possibility of remembering oneself by becoming a foreigner.

Here the question of the correct gesture doubles back on itself. For the artist, the correct gesture, barely perceptible on the screen, marks the gesture of the saint that resumes the line drawn by the event and its reminiscence. The question is one of mastery, of the *imperium* that the filmmaker exercises over the production of meaning. What is naturally evoked at the foot of the statue is the image of the filmmaker-*imperator* Eisenstein: he who moved statues, bronze horsemen or Odessa lions. But the distance between Eisenstein and Rossellini is immediately apparent: here mastery is not the art of animating stone in order to mark the downfall of the idols and the passage of History. Rather, in its absolute fragility, it is the irremediable exactitude of the gesture, the outline of the ineffaceable, in which the fulfilled destiny of the saint—the madwoman—and the success of the work—its cruelty—reflect one another.

For there are two figures of the irremediable. On the one hand, there are those that give weight to the social: the images filing past on the screen, the incessant movement of the assembly line: the cement bags in the factory, the pages spilling out of the go-betweens' rotary presses. The images and bags go by relentlessly. This is what is called reality. Unavoidable, they say. At most you should set aside the torn sack or the unclear image, shelve the explanation that has passed its day. On the other hand, what is irremediable in the work is the risk of there being no return, the cruelty taken on by the fiction: *a child kills himself*. Not "a child is being beaten," the fantasy of the family romance whose workings are explained by psychoanalysis. Still less the politicians' fiction of the massacre of the innocents that calls for inquiry and judgment. "A child kills himself" is the fiction of vertigo, the fiction that is crueler than any other—that is, the fiction of the work as cruelty: the stroke of the irremediable that cuts again and again into the pain of the family romance. Thus Rossellini has the child—the little Romano taken from him by illness—kill himself, throw himself into the void twice: first in the ruins of Berlin, and a second time in the Roman apartment that used to be but no longer is his. The limit-fiction is that of the work in general. For there to be a work, a child has to kill himself, a childhood has to be put to death. And the childhood that is put to death has to lose itself in the absolute risk of the work consecrated to the production of what is barely perceptible. The singular power of *Europe 51* consists in the exact conjunction between the cruelty of the fable and the cruelty of the work, in the coincidence represented between the work's fiction and its ethic. We should not understand this to mean the classical mastery that transforms the law of composition of the work into the subject of its fable, but rather the absolute dispossession that brings the scandal of sainthood and the perdition of the work back to their common origin and discrepancy: the material inscription of what has no place in the system of reality, the rigorously material dispensation of the immaterial that, in art as in religion, is called grace.

From the labor of the artist who wonders and asks us whether sainthood is still possible, there comes another question, a sister question concerning the possibility of the work: how can the incessant production of the social, the law of shock and interpretation, still authorize a work? What sort of cruelty can the artist still allow himself in a world that allows less and less place to atopia? I spoke about dates: the one that gives the film its title and that of a first viewing at the beginning of the 1960s. What was feverishly developing among us at that time was an activism convinced of the urgency of learning to read, see, listen, stop images and turn them around, and dig underneath words and between the lines—the moment of structuralism, the Marxist revival, semiology, and the new wave. Now, seeing this dated film of Rossellini's again today, this film of the postwar years—the age of the great humanist narratives and questions about the human condition and the destiny of the world, but also of the triumph of cinema as an art and means of expression—the film seems to attack us from the other side and point up that frenetic critique of words and images as a labor of mourning. As if we had started wanting to read and see, started learning to read and see only when such things were entirely taken up in the system of shock and interpretation and already had no more importance. Our generation staked its battle on the theme: stop the images, as if it were a question of courageously opposing their projection, the captivating shock of stimuli. But shock was already accompanied by interpretation; the couple was installed as a dominant system of representation, and no doubt our enthusiasm, even as we wanted to be critical, helped install it in this domination. We know today that criticism of images is vain because the image appears already escorted by its criticism, affected by its mark of distance and irony. In vain do well-meaning souls bemoan the fate of children who are stupefied by overexposure to televised images. But the child who watches television gets the socialized procedures of criticism at the same time he is assaulted by the shock of images. Training in the incessant production of images is also a training in criticism as a complementary social activity that derives from the same regime of representability. The flood of criticism is exactly contemporaneous with the flood of images. Demystification is part of stupefaction, of an investing the system of places and ways of occupying them that excludes only one thing: atopia.

Perhaps the duality, the divided destiny of the "new wave" of the 1960s can also be understood in this double scansion. On the one hand, the new wave represented a liberation of the camera, which became the witness of a universe in which figures, spaces, and codes were joyously cut loose from their moorings: running and sliding, disguises and pantomimes and ludicrous encounters, offscreen voices and false match cuts, white painted walls of apartments for young couples and Mediterranean honeymoons.... A particular kind of play was established between Godard's incongruous indoor cycling exercises and the Club-Méditerranée drunkenness of Corsica, where the camera of *Adieu Philippine* followed secretaries running away from the office and from morality: a particular communication between the iconoclastic ambition to undo the codes of representation, the relations between images and words, and the liberated morals of the new social figures advertising happiness: sun on demand and sex without worry. The new wave's devotion to Rossellini prevented us from seeing the gulf separating two universes and two regimes of representation. The liberated camera of the new wave both established and reflected a space where transversals became the norm; where incongruity took the place of the event, where drifting took the place of atopia and iconoclasm that of scandal. The figure of the foreigner who brings scandal with her, stepping off to the side, meeting with the unrepresentable, all fell back into the past and became incomprehensible to a generation that did not recognize any prohibited social or sexual relationship, any relation between words and images that could not be played upon within the frame of the continuous hustle and bustle of representation. Just as there were no sunny beaches where the Club could not take you in the middle of winter, there were no points of representation that could not be connected by a match cut. It was the time of the eternal possibility of a supplement: threesomes and match cuts. The mirage of the 1960s: that of a society governed only by the pleasure principle, in which, by the same measure, there was no longer any place for the work's cruelty: the cruelty of a child killing himself or that of a mother's perdition.

Of course the pleasure principle never reigns alone. On the other side of the impossible atopia, opposite the liberated image and the vagabond representation of new happiness in the winter sun, another figure of iconoclasm arose: no longer the pleasure of incongruity but the labor of criticism; no longer the freedom of representation but the suspension of representation, its exhibition on a screen turned into a blackboard, governed with circles and arrows, its tricks forever pointed out, the match cut played back over and over again to demonstrate its falsehood. No longer the guilt-free morality of grown-up children but the guilty politics of well-educated young militants, which never stops warning you to beware of the way words are tied to images and illustrates this with self-criticism. The best example of this is the path of Godard's career and the insistence of films like *Ici et ailleurs* on dismantling the traps of sound and image by which we love to be fooled. The pregnant Palestinian militant dedicating her child to the revolution was actually a Lebanese actress who was not expecting a child; if you could understand the language of the Palestinian guerrillas, you would know that they were not talking about the revolution or the class struggle, as the commentary overdubbed their words, but simply about where to cross the river.

However rigorous this pursuit of lies might be, who can fail to see its price? As the lie is tracked down, the truth gets reduced to the question of place, the certainty of the right place. The disappearance of the child, the going-astray of the mother were only the actress's lies—political and theatrical lies—in opposition to the authenticity of a place that found a way to speak itself in its own language. Thus was established an infinite deferment between an impossible morality of the camera and an impossible morality of politics. The passion to stop the image became the passion play of the work's death. As if the age of the work had come to an end with the age of scandal, closing, in the final image of *Europe 51*, with the gesture of benediction and farewell given by the foreigner, the saint, the madwoman. As if the moment of her imprisonment had begun the age of the absence of the work balanced between the hedonism of images and the archaeology of imprisonment; the age of mimetic radicalness, in which a certain idea of happiness and a certain idea of unhappiness can no longer find a meeting point; in which the work's labor of mourning can only be thought of as that which accompanies revolutions, before being thought of as the mourning for revolutions themselves.

Notes

INTRODUCTION

1. Yves Bonnefoy, "Paul Celan," *Le Nuage rouge* (Paris: Mercure de France, 1977), p. 304.

THE NEW LAND

1. Aldous Huxley, "Wordsworth in the Tropics," *Collected Essays* (New York: Harper and Row, 1959), pp. 1–10.
2. William Wordsworth, *The Prelude; or, Growth of a Poet's Mind* (1850 text), vi.357–59, ed. Ernest de Selincourt, 2d ed. (Oxford: Clarendon Press, 1959), p. 195.
3. Wordsworth, "French Revolution as It Appeared to Enthusiasts at Its Commencement," ll. 36–39, in *The Poetical Works of William Wordsworth*, ed. Ernest de Selincourt, 5 vols. (Oxford: Clarendon Press, 1944), vol. 2, p. 265.
4. Wordsworth, *Prelude*, vi.386–401, p. 197.
5. Ibid., vi.770–72, p. 219.
6. Wordsworth, *Descriptive Sketches* (1849 version), ll. 601–10, *Poetical Works*, vol. 1, p. 85.
7. Wordsworth, *Prelude*, ix.36–39, p. 317.
8. Ibid., ix.284–87, pp. 329–31.
9. Ibid., ix.300–302, p. 331.
10. Ibid., ix.311–13, p. 331.

11. Ibid., ix.404–7, p. 337.

12. Ibid., ix.67–80, p. 319.

13. Wordsworth, *The Borderers* (1797–99 version), IV.ii. 144–45, ed. Robert Osborn (Ithaca, N.Y.: Cornell University Press, 1982), p. 238.

14. Ibid., II.iii.337–44, p. 172.

15. Wordsworth, "To the Clouds," ll. 53–57, *Poetical Works*, vol. 2, pp. 318–19.

16. Wordsworth, Postscript (1835) to *Lyrical Ballads*, *Poetical Works*, vol. 2, p. 449.

17. Wordsworth, "Lucy Gray," *Poetical Works*, vol. 1, pp. 234–36; "We Are Seven," *Poetical Works*, vol. 1, pp. 236–38; "There Was a Boy," *Poetical Works*, vol. 2, pp. 318–19.

18. See Collin, Rogé, Maréchal, Charpin, Lamy, *L'Année de la mère: Mission de l'est* (Toulon: Imprimerie de Canquoin, 1833). On the Saint-Simonian missionaries, see Jacques Rancière, *The Nights of Labor: The Workers' Dream in Nineteenth-Century France*, trans. John Drury (Philadelphia: Temple University Press, 1989).

19. Letter from Michel Chevalier to Hoart and Bruneau, November 26, 1832, Bibliothèque de l'Arsenal, Fonds Enfantin, Ms. 7646. All translations of secondary sources are by the translator of this volume, unless otherwise indicated.

20. Letter from Cayol to Michel Chevalier, December 20, 1832, Fonds Enfantin, Ms. 7647.

21. Letter from Hoart to Henry-René Picard, January 9, 1833, cited in Henry-René d'Allemagne, *Les Saint-simoniens* (Paris: Gründ, 1930), p. 367.

22. Memoirs of Jean Terson, Fonds Enfantin, Ms. 7787.

23. Letter from Hoart to Picard, in d'Allemagne, *Les Saint-simoniens*, p. 366.

24. Memoirs of Terson.

25. Letter from Bruneau to Ollivier, n.d., Fonds Enfantin, Ms. 7647.

NOTES 137

26. Letter from Ollivier to Prosper Enfantin, n.d., Fonds Enfantin.

27. Letter from Émile Barrault to Enfantin, February 21, 1833, Fonds Enfantin.

28. Letter from Jules Mercier to Julien Gallé, n.d., *Livre des actes* (Paris: Alexandre Johanneau, 1833), p. 35.

29. Collin et al., *L'Année de la mère*, p. 19.

30. Ibid., pp. 19–20.

31. Ibid., pp. 20–22.

32. Ibid., p. 23.

33. Ibid., pp. 30–31.

34. Ibid., p. 31.

35. Georg Büchner to his family, May 1833, *Werke und Briefe*, ed. Warner R. Lehmann et al. (Munich: DTV, 1980), pp. 249–50.

36. "August Becker's Testimony About Büchner's and Weidig's Political Activities," in *Georg Büchner: The Complete Collected Works*, trans. Henry J. Schmidt (New York: Avon, 1977), pp. 262–63. For a complete dossier on the *Hessian Messenger*, see Gerhard Schaub, *Georg Büchner, "Der Hessische Landbote": Texte, Materialen, Kommentar* (Munich: Carl Hanser Verlag, 1976).

37. Quote from Büchner to Karl Gutzkow, Georg Büchner, *Complete Plays, Lenz, and Other Writings*, trans. John Reddick (Harmondsworth, Eng.: Penguin, 1993), p. 200.

38. Büchner, *Danton's Death*, I.i, *Complete Plays*, p. 5.

39. "A mistake crept in when we were made, there's something missing, I don't know what it is, we'll never discover it by groping around in each other's guts, so why smash open each other's bodies to try to find it?" (ibid., II.i, p. 29).

40. Ibid.

41. Büchner to Gutzkow, [1836], *Complete Plays*, pp. 204–5.

42. Büchner to Gutzkow, *Complete Plays*, p. 201.

43. Büchner, *Woyzeck*, *Complete Plays*, pp. 133–34.

44. Büchner, *Leonce and Lena*, II.ii, *Complete Plays*, p. 96.

45. Büchner to his family, Zurich, November 20, 1836, *Complete Plays*, p. 206.

46. Büchner to Minna Jaeglé, Zurich, January 20, 1837, *Complete Plays*, p. 207.

47. Achille Rousseau, *La Magdeleine* (Paris: Bufquin-Désessart, 1835), pp. 206–7.

48. Büchner to his family, January 1, 1836, *Werke und Briefe*, p. 279.

49. Büchner to Jaeglé, *Complete Plays*, p. 208.

50. Eugène Bonnemère, *Le roman de l'avenir* (Paris: Librairie Internationale, 1869), p. iii.

51. Claude Genoux, *Mémoires d'un enfant de la Savoie* (Paris: G. Barba, 1844), p. 206.

52. Ibid., p. 182.

53. Ibid., p. 166.

54. Ibid., pp. 7–8.

55. *L'Atelier* 6, no. 12 (September 1846): 383–84. *L'Atelier* was published in Paris from 1840 to 1847.

56. Genoux, *Mémoires*, p. 230.

THE POOR WOMAN

1. Paul Viallaneix, preface to Jules Michelet, *Journal*, 4 vols. (Paris: Gallimard, 1959–76), vol. 2, pp. xvii–xviii.

2. Michelet, *Journal*, July 21, 1842, vol. 1, p. 457.

3. Michelet, notes for a course at the Collège de France, 1843, cited in Paul Viallaneix, *La Voie royale: Essai sur l'idée du peuple dans l'œuvre de Michelet* (Paris: Flammarion, 1971), p. 50.

4. Michelet, "L'Héroisme de l'esprit," *L'Arc* 52 (1973): 13.

5. Michelet, 1843 course notes, Viallaneix, *La Voie royale*, p. 51.

6. Michelet, *Journal*, January 20, 1843, vol. 1, p. 497.

7. Ibid., November 2, 1844, vol. 1, pp. 582–83.

8. Viallaneix, *La Voie royale*, p. 48.

9. Michelet, *Origines du droit français*, *Œuvres complètes*,

ed. Paul Viallaneix, 21 vols. (Paris: Flammarion, 1973–85), vol. 3, p. 607.

10. Michelet, *Du prêtre, de la femme, et de la famille* (Paris: Hachette, Paulin, 1845), p. 272.

11. Michelet, *La Femme, Œuvres complètes*, vol. 18, p. 400.

12. Michelet, *L'Amour, Œuvres complètes*, vol. 18, p. 58.

13. Michelet, *La Femme*, p. 421.

14. Ibid., p. 415.

15. Michelet, *L'Amour*, p. 220.

16. Rainer Maria Rilke, *The Notebooks of Malte Laurids Brigge*, trans. Stephen Mitchell (New York: Vintage International, 1990), p. 7.

17. Rilke to Marie von Thurn und Taxis, March 21, 1913, *The Letters of Rainer Maria Rilke and Princess Marie von Thurn und Taxis*, trans. Nora Wydenbruck (London: Hogarth Press, 1958), p. 91. The italicized passages here and in other citations from Rilke's correspondence are in French in the original.

18. Ibid.; cf. the same image in Rilke, *Stories of God*, trans. M. D. Herter Norton (New York: W. W. Norton, 1963), p. 58.

19. Cf. Jacques Rancière, *The Nights of Labor: The Workers' Dream in Nineteenth-Century France*, trans. John Drury (Philadelphia: Temple University Press, 1989).

20. Rilke to von Thurn und Taxis, March 21, 1913, *Letters of Rilke and von Thurn und Taxis*, p. 92.

21. Ibid.

22. Rilke, *The Book of Hours: Prayers to a Lowly God*, trans. Annemarie S. Kidder (Evanston, Ill.: Northwestern University Press, 2001), p. 201.

23. Ibid., p. 193.

24. Ibid., p. 197.

25. Rilke to Magda von Hattingberg (Benvenuta), February 4, 1914, *Rilke and Benvenuta: An Intimate Correspondence*, trans. Joel Agee (New York: Fromm, 1987), p. 12. On the same theme, see in particular the beginning of *The Book of*

Poverty and Death, as well as Marie von Thurn und Taxis, *Memoirs of a Princess*, trans. Nora Wydenbruck (London: Hogarth Press, 1959), p. 178.

26. Rilke to von Thurn und Taxis, March 21, 1913, *Letters of Rilke and von Thurn und Taxis*, p. 92. Translation modified.

27. Rilke, *Sonnets to Orpheus*, I, 19, *Ahead of All Parting: The Selected Poetry and Prose of Rainer Maria Rilke*, trans. Stephen Mitchell (New York: Modern Library, 1995), p. 447.

28. Rilke to von Hattingberg, February 13, 1914, *Rilke and Benvenuta*, pp. 49–50.

29. Ibid., February 24, 1914, p. 127.

30. Rilke, *Sonnets to Orpheus*, I, 9, *Ahead of All Parting*, p. 427.

31. Pierre-Joseph Proudhon, *Du principe de l'art et de sa destination sociale* (Paris: Garnier Frères, 1865), p. 335.

32. Rilke, *Sonnets to Orpheus*, II, 16, and II, 19, *Ahead of All Parting*, pp. 493 and 499.

33. Ibid., I, 11, p. 431.

34. Rilke to Countess M., September 26, 1919, *Letters of Rainer Maria Rilke*, trans. Jane Bannard Greene and M. D. Herter Norton, 2 vols. (New York: W. W. Norton, 1947), vol. 2, p. 207.

35. Rilke to von Thurn und Taxis, January 18, 1920, *Letters of Rilke and von Thurn und Taxis*, p. 182.

36. Rilke to Lou Salomé, January 16, 1920, *Rainer Maria Rilke/Lou Andreas-Salomé: Briefwechsel*, ed. Ernst Pfeiffer (Frankfurt am Main: Insel Verlag, 1975), p. 418.

A CHILD KILLS HIMSELF

1. Alain Bergala, "Roberto Rossellini et l'invention du cinéma moderne," preface to Roberto Rossellini, *Le Cinéma révélé* (Paris: Éditions de l'Étoile, 1984), p. 11.

2. Cf. Jacques Rancière, "La Chute des corps: Physique de Rossellini," *La Fable cinématographique* (Paris: Éditions du Seuil, 2001), pp. 165–85.

3. Louis Althusser, "From *Capital* to Marx's Philosophy," Louis Althusser and Etienne Balibar, *Reading Capital*, trans. Ben Brewster (London: Verso, 1979), pp. 15–17.

4. In Greek: *Ea chaïreïn*, an expression habitually used by Plato at certain strategic moments of the Socratic dialogues, in particular *Phaedo* 63c and *Phaedrus* 230a.

5. Plato, *Phaedrus* 229c.

6. Gabriel Gauny, *Le Philosophe plébien* (Paris: La Découverte/Presses Universitaires de Vincennes, 1983), p. 52.

7. Hyppolite Taine, *Italy: Rome and Naples*, trans. J. Durand (New York: Leypoldt and Holt, 1869), pp. 109–10.

Atopia: Philosophy, Political Theory, Aesthetics

Branka Arsic, *Gaze and Subjectivity in Berkeley (via Beckett)*

Jacques Rancière, *Short Voyages to the Land of the People*

Béatrice Han, *Foucault's Critical Project: Between the Transcendental and the Historical*

Gregg M. Horowitz, *Sustaining Loss: Art and Mournful Life*

Robert Gooding-Williams, *Zarathustra's Dionysian Modernism*

Denise Riley, *The Words of Selves: Identification, Solidarity, Irony*

James Swenson, *On Jean-Jacques Rousseau: Considered as One of the First Authors of the Revolution*